Leadership

ON PURPOSE

How Agile Leaders Inspire Others

**Michael P. Grubich
and Shelley A. Smith**

Title: Leadership ON PURPOSE: How Agile Leaders Inspire Others
Copyright© 2021 Michael P. Grubich and Shelley A. Smith.

For information regarding permission to reprint material from this book, please mail or email your request to mgrubich@lak-group.com or ssmith@lak-group.com.

ISBN: (Paperback)

ADVANCE PRAISE

"What a comprehensive and fresh book on Leadership! Mike and Shelley have developed a thorough, actionable, yet succinct model for Agile Leadership. This book pinpoints the essential leadership qualities for today's leaders at every level. It's rich with great personal stories, an amalgamation of relevant research, and both fictional and historic examples that bring the principles to life. I especially appreciate the excellent research and extensive references provided. Bottom line — it's a great guide for truly understanding and then choosing to lead *on purpose*."

> — Mina Brown, President and Founder, Coach Academy International

"Leadership is a journey with beautiful sunrises, new and exciting experiences and, at times, challenging terrain to navigate. This practical book – through its stories and thought-provoking questions – made me think deeply not only about my leadership journey that brought me to where I am today, but also how by leading on purpose, I can be a better leader for those I will have the privilege to work in the miles ahead."

> — Amy Rislov, Chief Human Resources Officer, Sentry Insurance

"*Leadership* ON PURPOSE, by Michael Grubich and Shelley Smith, is a wonderful read for anyone interested in the art, science and practice of leadership. Leaders of any experience and at any level will discover new principles to apply in their daily work. Michael and Shelley have created a handbook dedicated to the belief that leadership can be taught and always improved. And when it is, it makes a world of difference. I can't wait to use it with my team of leaders!"

> — Mary Jo Cagle, MD and Chief Operating Officer, Cone Health

"Wow! What a cornucopia of information, best practices and practical encouragement! This book is resource-rich. For those who want to go deeper into the various attributes of On Purpose Leaders, there are dozens of additional resources cited throughout. This book could very well be your first step on a journey of a thousand miles."

> — Susan A. Marshall, Founder, Backbone Institute, LLC

"I found *Leadership ON PURPOSE* to be refreshingly integrative and quite practical for aspiring leaders and organizations wanting to improve. Michael Grubich and Shelley Smith's book is accessible, lively, and contains useful applications to strengthen leaders and help organizations optimize their futures."

—Mark A. Mone, PhD, Chancellor, University of Wisconsin-Milwaukee

"Leadership *ON PURPOSE* is a fresh new view of leadership that is even more important during these challenging, stressful times."

—John Cayer, President, Mueller Sports Medicine

DEDICATION

This book is dedicated to current and future leaders …

~ who are driven by purpose and have a hunger to make a lasting impact on the lives of others.

~ who desire to become the kind of leader that people are inspired to follow, voluntarily.

~ who are willing to give their strength to others so that they may have the strength to stand on their own.

~ who are humble enough to understand their gaps and have the courage to make a change.

~ who intentionally choose their happiness and are able to derive satisfaction from the success of others.

COVER ART MEANING

A great deal of thought went into the cover art of our book. We wanted to be intentional about it and have the artwork, in and of itself, convey a message.

Our book delves into many of the thoughts, behaviors, beliefs, and actions of leaders who are agile and Lead *On Purpose*. The photograph signifies many of those elements.

The image epitomizes change, adaptability, agility, and reflection. Leaves change color as the seasons change. Trees lose their leaves at the end of each year and then grow them back in the spring. All the while, the lake's reflection captures the true and accurate image of the events as they unfold.

As leaders, we need to be able to adapt as events change. We need to act with purpose, agility, and resiliency as we grow, as well as when we lose people, money, or stability. We also need to be able to see the reflection of our leadership as others see it – not as we want it to be.

Photo by Nick Schroeter Photography: www.ns-photo.com

CONTENTS

ACKNOWLEDGEMENTS

This book would not have been possible without the trust and confidence others had in us. Throughout the years, our experience working closely with leaders and organizations has challenged and helped develop our capabilities as leaders.

The work we have done, the projects we have been a part of, the situations we have faced, and the partners we have worked with have all contributed to our ongoing journey to becoming better Agile Leaders and to our passion for Leading *On Purpose*.

A special thank you to those that have supported us on our journeys to help others find their purpose and clarify their intentions in leading others. We have been influenced by so many people and will be forever grateful for their influence and contributions.

We are especially grateful for our colleagues at LAK Group. We talk about acting *On Purpose* through this book, and we are very lucky to work with wonderful, talented professionals who are committed to purpose and providing the best experience possible for our clients.

Finally, we want to acknowledge the support of our families and close friends for the love and encouragement given to us throughout our careers. Knowing you were always there for us makes both this journey and the destination worthwhile.

PREFACE

We believe that it's not the position that makes the leader, but the leader that makes the position. The intent of the organization must be to cultivate leaders who want to Lead *On Purpose*. The culture of the team, organization, and community, is driven by the behavior of leaders. What is the answer to the timeless question: "Are leaders born or developed?" We think it's both.

Leadership is a privilege. It is a gift given to others to help them have a positive impact on the organization. Leaders can certainly change organizations, but more importantly, they can change lives. Leadership comes with high expectations and immense accountability. People look to leaders to help them succeed or to resolve problems. They count on leaders to focus on the greater good of the organization and its people. They want leaders who act *On Purpose*.

Throughout our careers, we have worked for a number of great organizations and experienced both good and "not so good" leaders. Through our journeys, we have come to realize that there is one common variable that separates great organizations from the rest: Agile Leaders who are driven by the impact they have on others. Our purpose is to highlight the key attributes that differentiate great leaders. This leads to sustainable business results, organizations that are able to adapt to changing market conditions, and people who are change resilient.

The goal of any organization of any size must be the successful development of strong, Agile Leaders at all levels. The intent must be to cultivate those who inspire others, encourage creativity and innovation, and have the capacity to build change-resilience in others.

These Agile Leaders must possess an inner drive that is energized when translating complex situations that require clear and specific actions to be taken. They must be internally motivated to want to create higher engagement, more trust, and stronger relationships among employees, customers, and other constituents.

The evolution of great leaders requires experiences, learning, and reflection. This includes taking on difficult situations, adapting, and learning from those challenges. Additionally, great leaders have a passion for impacting and inspiring others. They don't do it for the money, glory, title, status, or recognition. They become leaders because they feel that it is their purpose – some have told us that they see it as their destiny.

We hope this is not simply another leadership book. Our hope is that you can take action to improve your capability based on the practical examples and tools we have included. The key truly comes as you look inside yourself and ask the questions, "Why do I want to be a leader?" and "What kind of leader do I want to be?" How you answer these questions will help you to begin your personal journey to Leadership *On Purpose*. We hope you will find value in and enjoy reading our contribution.

INTRODUCTION

There is no denying the dramatic changes that have confronted organizations in recent years. Ongoing advancements in technology and automation alone have altered the business model of many companies, prompting them to modify their operations and processes in order to keep pace and stay competitive.

Adding to those challenges now and accelerating change across all facets of business has been the COVID-19 pandemic. Many organizations have downsized considerably while others have been forced to find different ways of keeping their new or expanded workforce active and engaged. Leaders are faced with the challenge of managing and leading a workforce that is partially or completely remote. Moreover, leaders and employees alike are faced with new health concerns, home education, and safety and security challenges no one could have anticipated.

While the times and events may have impacted organizations and their leaders, the overarching objectives are still the same: achieve organizational goals, keep employees engaged and involved, and continue to attract and retain top talent. The solutions will vary. Many will invest in various work-from-home technologies; others will cut expenses or modify or drop processes and product lines to find greater efficiencies; and many will cut staff or ask their staff to do more with less.

What's the right answer? Only the individual organization knows. However, we argue that without the development of the leaders within the organization, positive results will increasingly become more difficult to achieve.

Constant and disruptive change has accelerated the need for leaders who possess a purpose-driven, agile mindset, an ability to create followership, and a trustworthiness that instills resiliency, optimism, and confidence in others. In our research and practice, we have discovered that dealing with change of any kind is all about leadership and having leaders who lead with purpose. Purpose is a word that's used in many different contexts. Our use of it is two-fold:

Leadership *On Purpose* means having an intention – a reason for wanting to be a leader that is above and beyond personal gain. It's about your leadership presence and your mindfulness of the actions you take and in the words you use. It's displaying congruence between intention and behavior.

Being *On Purpose* also means being self-aware of *why* you do what you do. It's an acceptance of the path to be the kind of purpose-driven leader and person you want to be.

It's stepping up to the plate and being accountable for what's required of you in order to make positive change happen through yourself and others.

Leaders *On Purpose* set vision first, then influence and inspire others to opt-in, share in that vision, and discover how their efforts fit into the greater goal. Leaders with an intent of this nature challenge and inspire every person (leaders and individual contributors alike) to be a part of something greater, to insert themselves into the story, and to take accountability for their role.

We define these individuals as Agile Leaders – those who others trust and rally around. Agile Leaders possess a leadership mindset that's purpose-based and other-oriented, rather than results-based or only intended to satisfy a self-interest. Agile Leaders cast a positive shadow that often endures well beyond their time in office. They serve as a catalyst for change and change-resilience and as an anchor for an organization's core principals and direction.

Throughout our careers, we have worked with many organizations and many different types of leaders. We have been a part of culture-shaping work, restructuring, talent management initiatives, leadership development efforts, engagement efforts, upsizing, downsizing, rightsizing, and change management. We have also been leaders ourselves – of processes, departments, functions, and people. And it is from this experience that we have arrived at the concepts and models that we will share with you in this book.

When we started our journey, we were purposeful in not wanting our contribution to be "another leadership book." We wanted it to be different. We believe that our experiences, lessons learned, and blended perspectives offer a distinct view of leadership. You see, we believe that anyone can be a leader, with or without a title. We believe that real leaders are the ones who are noticed, respected, and followed by others, regardless of their position or title. Their intentions and behaviors signify to others that they have accepted the role of leadership for reasons other than personal gain. Leaders *On Purpose* achieve success as a result of their ability to enhance the success of others. This is our definition of being successful in leadership.

To us, it's not a question of whether leaders are born or developed. We believe that some individuals are more natural at leadership than others. We believe that leading well can be accomplished by anyone with an "other-oriented" mindset and the willingness and agility to learn and grow.

In our research on the effectiveness of leaders in global and domestic organizations, we have identified six attributes that are unfailingly present in Agile Leaders and are of the utmost importance for purpose-driven leaders to possess in order to inspire and develop others and ensure the sustainability and success of their organizations. We have also found that these attributes are essential for mid-level leaders to acquire so that they can effectively unite and align every function of an organization and enable it to achieve its business objectives. *The Six Attributes of an Agile Leader* include:

Personal Integrity – your presence as a leader.

Learning Agility – your ability and willingness to learn from experience.

Coaching Others – accepting accountability for the development of others.

Followership – your talent to inspire, build credibility, and earn the trust of others.

Systems Thinking – your capacity to view the organization from a broader perspective.

Change Resiliency – your ability to maintain consistent personal integrity and a level of productivity through a variety of situations.

Why does all of this matter? As we shared at the onset, organizations today are trying everything they can to maintain cultures that can contend with disruptive change. They need Agile Leaders with vision and an intention for growth who can build and sustain followership and inspire and support their people through these changing times. They need Agile Leaders to create an organizational culture that is confident and optimistic in the face of change, engaged, aligned in purpose, and centered on achieving its business objectives.

This all matters because culture change is not an initiative or specific activity that you can deploy. Not if you want it to stick. A positive, engaged, and productive culture is the outcome of your intent, capability, and presence as a leader. It's the result of your cumulative and repetitive actions and the impact of your actions on the mindset and engagement of others.

As we embark on the beginning of a new year – whether by the calendar or just by beginning a new day – and learn to embrace the changes and uncertainties around us, we ask that you read the chapters that follow and reflect on your own goals, actions, behaviors, and intentions as a leader.

We invite you to consider how in line your intentions and purpose are with *On Purpose* leadership. We also invite you to reflect on the ways in which you can become even better at what you do, in order to make a difference in the lives of others and in the sustained success of your organization.

Within these chapters, we provide you with the rationale and roadmap, tips, and techniques for developing *The Six Attributes of Agile Leaders.* These qualities will help you as a leader to create cultures that attract, inspire, and retain top talent. We hope that you'll find the stories, processes, and thought models supportive in your journey to becoming an Agile Leader and that they help to encourage the development of Agile Leaders at all levels within your organization.

Our hope is that this is not just another leadership book for your bookshelf or Kindle library. We encourage you to write in the margins, dog ear page corners, highlight text, and use sticky notes. We want this to be the book you reference, the thought models you default to, and the techniques you apply to become an even better and stronger leader who leads *On Purpose* and succeeds through the success of others.

1
LEADING *ON PURPOSE*

*The heart of human excellence often begins to beat when you discover a pursuit
that absorbs you, frees you, challenges you, or gives you a sense of
meaning, joy, or passion.*

—*Terry Orlick*

"Where do you hope to be in five years?" It's a common question asked during interviews and goal setting conversations with employees. "I hope to be in a leadership position" or "I hope to be promoted to a vice president role" are not uncommon answers. When asked why they want to achieve that position, their usual answers include: *"Because I want to be in charge;" "Because I want to be the boss;" "Because I will make more money;" "Because I've been told that I am good at what I do and that is the next step for my career;"* and the most common, *"It is the obvious next step for my career."*

Unfortunately, while all of these are most likely genuine answers, they're not the right answers when it comes to pursuing what we term: Leadership *On Purpose*.

"Because I want to be in charge" expresses a desire for control and oversight of others;

"Because I want to be the boss" expresses a motivation to run the show;

"Because I want more money" is a motivation for self-benefit; and,

"Because I am told that I am good at what I do and that's the next step for my career" is a statement that serves oneself while appeasing others.

Leaders need to want to be leaders for the right reasons, that is, reasons that are less centered on self and self-advancement and more focused on the advancement of others and the organization.

Our belief is that to have what it takes to be a leader who others truly want to follow, one must have a leadership mindset that is purpose-based. Moreover, Leaders *On Purpose* have two aims that must intertwine: one is pursuing a leadership role with an intention; the other is ensuring that one's vision, plans, actions, and behaviors align with the goals of the organization. Leaders aren't simply born and developed – they have a mindset that believes their purpose is to positively impact the lives of others.

Many extremely talented individuals aspire to leadership roles, only to find once they arrive that they are no longer able to concentrate on and do what they do best. They realize, often too late, that the role of a leader is completely different from what they had expected, what motivates them, and what they are skilled to do. We've experienced this outcome in every organization we've worked with.

One such organization was a global leader in equipment manufacturing where Mike was the global head of Human Resources for new product development. To design the innovative products demanded by the changing market, the enterprise needed to build out their electronics expertise and capabilities. The first step was finding someone to lead that group.

The first person placed in the leadership role was one of the emerging leaders in the organization, a highly-skilled electronics engineer who had tremendous success with design innovation, margins, and market share. Yet, this turned out to be a poor decision for both the organization and the chosen leader. While in the new position, he kept letting himself get involved in the design tactics. He kept spending his time on technical matters and not leading and building his team. He couldn't separate himself from his passion and talent as an engineer. This inhibited his ability to build the organization and lead the team.

The next person to take on that role was Tom, someone fortunately found internally. Tom wasn't necessarily the best electronics engineer, He did, however, demonstrate the qualities and attributes of leadership. And although he wasn't as technically skilled as the other members of his team, and was actually being paid less than most of his engineers, he was able to build a very strong, united, and focused group of skilled professionals.

Tom wanted that role for a reason. It wasn't about the title or attaining credit for being at the helm when the team's engineering designs led to patents. He knew that purposeful leadership would be important if the organization was to excel in its capability and expertise.

Tom learned the meaning of leadership while growing up on a farm. He learned to balance what he did with what other family members and the seasonal help did so there was complement and no overlap. He knew that he couldn't do everything on his own. He learned when, where, and how to jump in and do things himself, and when to have confidence in someone else jumping in. He had a genuine level of humility that was and is the foundation of his character and demeanor.

He led the team of engineers brilliantly because he did it for the good of the product, his people, the customer, and the organization … a greater purpose. He knew his role was not to design the most innovative technology. That was his team's role. His role was to guide and support his team of innovative engineers by removing any roadblocks and inspiring their performance.

John C. Maxwell notably said, *"Leadership is not about titles, positions, or flowcharts. It is about one life influencing another."* This is what we mean when we talk about Leadership *On Purpose*. Tom had the character traits, behaviors, and skills to be the leader of that engineering team. Moreover, he had the right purpose – the growth and success of his team.

It is our belief that Leaders *On Purpose* serve the greater good of self, others, and the organization. A leader who establishes a vision and set goals, develops new things for the value and prosperity of others, and unites the organization in that quest is Leading *On Purpose*.

It *Is* About Mindset

Mindset is a concept that has received a lot of attention in the last decade, though research regarding the subject has been steady and on-going for much longer. Mindset can be described as an attitude or state of mind; an inclination, disposition, or mood; or simply a way of thinking. The reality is that our mindset has a direct bearing on our beliefs and on the actions we take.

Leading *On Purpose* requires, what Carol Dweck, author of *Mindset: The New Psychology of Success*, refers to as a "Growth Mindset."[1] Contrary to a "Fixed Mindset," which views situations, events, or individuals as being unchangeable and simply manageable, a leader with a Growth Mindset believes that each situation is nothing more than a starting point, and their role as a leader is being present at its beginning, not at its end.

Having a Growth Mindset as a leader enables you to bring in other people and other ideas that you might not have brought in at the inception of a concept or plan and enables you to brainstorm unique options and perhaps find new solutions. It guides you to reflect on the future impact of a decision beyond its immediate results.

Another distinction between a Fixed and Growth Mindset is in how one approaches challenges and disruptions. Ask yourself, when a challenge arises in your work or what you're trying to accomplish, do you immediately view it as a stopper or a starter? When you come across a barrier in your life, does it hold you back and make you stall or give up, or does it energize you to find a way to break through and move forward, regardless of the obstacle?

Someone who embodied this distinction in all facets of her life was Madame Curie, the famous 19th century physicist and chemist known for her pioneering research on radioactivity. She coined the term "radioactive." She was the first woman to win a Nobel Prize, the first person – and the only woman – to win the Nobel Prize twice, and the only person to win the Nobel Prize in two different scientific fields (chemistry and physics). She was also the first woman to become a professor at the University of Paris.[2]

Marie Curie faced numerous challenges and barriers throughout her lifetime, beginning with her endeavor to attain an advanced education as a female in her time. And the barriers were intense to her attempts to introduce the new element, radium, to the periodic table because many scientists at the time did not believe that radium was a new element at all.

In spite of her outstanding work and discoveries, because she was a woman, she continued to struggle for recognition within the French scientific community that didn't even allow her to speak at scientific conferences. This didn't deter Curie from finding breakthroughs in her work though.

As a leader, having a Growth Mindset about yourself, others, and the organization is extremely important for being agile and influential. It is a foundation for our Six Attributes of Agile Leaders that we will be highlighting later in this book. You need to be focused on how you're going to help others to be successful while also having a positive impact on their career, the organization, and their colleagues. The success of each member of your team and the overall organization is your responsibility. It is a heavy burden, but one that will add tremendous career and personal satisfaction if you operate with purpose. When you move into a leadership role, it's not about you any longer. It's about everyone else.

Leading *On Purpose* is as much an individual's choice as it is an organization's choice. Organizations need to make decisions around talent with purpose and individuals need to opt in to leading – whether formally or informally – with an intent and desire to learn. Part of that choice is how you define yourself as a leader and how you write yourself into the story.

Writing Yourself into the Story

There's another dynamic that compels people to move into leadership positions. Many times, newly-minted leaders arrive with the attitude, "I'm going to fix it," "I'm going to change the world," "I am not going to make the mistakes others have made," or "I am going to take this business and the team to new heights!"

They're locked in to a mindset where they are going to do everything opposite of what their bosses and others in the organization have done in the past. They often go down the path of an "I will show you" or "I got this" attitude, without stepping back to assess how their actions fit into the bigger picture of their team or the organization. We like to use a phrase that simply states: to lead change and truly shape culture, you need to write yourself into the story.

This is all about purpose, about setting a vision first and then influencing others to adopt that vision. It's about getting others to opt in and discover how their role and all of their efforts fit into that purpose. It challenges and inspires every person (leader or not) to take accountability for defining how they are going to establish themselves into the story of the organization.

The leadership team at Southwest Airlines provides a great example of creating a culture of exceptional service with a purpose that involves every single employee. They set out to change the dynamic of how airline service was delivered to the flying public and to drive a deeper intention into their approach to building customer loyalty.

Co-founder, and later CEO and chairman emeritus of Southwest Airlines until his death in 2019, Herbert Kelleher and his leadership team knew that in order to achieve their purpose, they needed to give their employees accountability and flexibility.[3]

At Southwest, flight attendants, baggage handlers, pilots, and hosts do everything they can to help each passenger smile and enjoy their trip. Whether through a humorous approach to reviewing safety procedures, by dancing in the aisle, or by singing a song during pre-flight announcements, they find and perform their particular role and character, and thereby write themselves individually into the Southwest story.[4]

Another example of a company where employees are empowered to write themselves into the story every day is the Ritz-Carlton. For years, the Ritz has been known as one of the gold standards of customer service. Business books have been written just on the Ritz's customer service alone. This is best demonstrated by their famous motto, "We are ladies and gentlemen serving ladies and gentlemen." One of the most effective elements is the authorization the Ritz puts directly into the hands of its employees. Each employee is empowered to spend up to $2,000 per incident to solve a customer's problem, without asking for a manager's intervention.[5] Ritz employees are encouraged to take the lead, have the authority, and ultimately feel the gratification of seeing a patron's needs met and often exceeded. They write themselves into the company story.

As a leader, many of the challenges you face include: how you are going to write yourself into your company's story; what you want your leadership legacy to be; and how you are going to help others write themselves into the story.

The Four C's of Leading *On Purpose*

When we first started working on our book, we identified four threads that surfaced in every writing session. We call them the *Four C's of Leading On Purpose*. In our experience, if you accept a leadership position, you'll need confidence, competence, courage, and curiosity in order to achieve your purpose: confidence in yourself and others; competence in talents and skills that are different than what brought you to your leadership role; courage in taking a stand for your ideas and that of your teammates; and a genuine curiosity to learn and grow as a leader, to give voice to others, and to grow the organization.

We present our *Four C's of Leading On Purpose* together in Chapter 1 because of their unique relationship: they each both compliment and depend on the other.

Confidence

Shelley worked with a leader who had just moved into the healthcare industry. The leader was faced with a challenge she had never been confronted with before – all of the management roles she had previously held were of a team or function for which she had a solid level of knowledge and experience. If help was needed, she could roll up her sleeves and fill most any role.

Yet, the leader's first role as a director in the specialized field of healthcare made her question her confidence. For the first time in her career, she couldn't fill in for her teammates. Being able to do that was her metric for confidence. She didn't have the training and discipline in dealing with people's health issues; she didn't have the proper licenses anyway; and quite honestly, she didn't have the stomach to do what many of her team members did. She needed to find confidence in her role as their director and in her ability to fill that role in ways that would not just benefit her, but would benefit her teammates and the organization as a whole.

She was soon reminded that one of her most important roles was to show confidence in her team and in their ability to perform their jobs. Equally important was for her to display confidence in her primary role as their director, which was to support them in their work and remove any obstacles to their performance.

Why is it so important to demonstrate confidence as a leader and what should a leader be confident about? Leadership confidence is about image, presence, and perceived ability. Confidence impacts a leader's ability to influence others and signals strength and accuracy in a leader's decision-making abilities. Confidence encourages leaders to challenge the status quo, to take risks, and to accomplish goals that would be otherwise unattainable.

People are not inclined to follow leaders who show hesitation, anxiety, and uncertainty. Fear, as a negative power, can be quite contagious. So is confidence, though as a more positive, productive force. As Steve Kerr, coach of the Golden State Warriors, puts it, "Your team needs to see you as confident."[6] Even if you don't feel confident inside, you still need to display confidence to your team.

As a leader, you need to have confidence in how you add value – which is very different from the value you add in a non-leadership position. As a leader, you add value through your resilience, your ability to influence others, your response when mistakes are made, and most especially, through your display of confidence in yourself and others.

Basketball legend Michael Jordan radiated Leadership *On Purpose*. Jordan's mindset was to first be at his best before he could lead others to their best and the Bulls franchise to its best:

> *"To be successful you have to be selfish, or else you never achieve. And once you get to your highest level, then you have to be unselfish. Stay reachable. Stay in touch. Don't isolate."*[7]

Jordan stepping into the role of leader – not just the Bull's superstar player – strengthened the team's culture. The trust Jordan literally placed in his teammates' hands during the big games showed that he valued them as basketball players and as people.

Leadership transformed Jordan. In his early years, when the score was close at the end of a game, Jordan always wanted the ball. But later, as a leader, he trusted his teammates to make the big play during several crucial playoff games.

The confidence that Michael Jordan instilled in his teammates and the performance that confidence made possible was the catalyst that transformed him from being a great player to becoming a basketball legend, and turned the Chicago Bulls into one of the most successful NBA franchises in basketball history.

Competence

The second thread of leadership is competence, but not as a subject matter expert or in one's ability to perform a day-to-day job. We're speaking of competence in leading people. This involves communicating, inspiring others, developing others, strategizing, and visioning. The truth is, as a leader, you need to have more competence around the bigger picture and how things are connected than around the process and tactics.

A lot of surveys and 360-degree employee evaluations ask, "What do you like about your leader?" The response is often, "She's not afraid to get her hands dirty." Unfortunately, many employees and their leaders believe this is what leadership is all about, when in fact "rolling up your sleeves" is one of the subtle myths about leadership.

Yes, you want leaders who aren't afraid to get their hands dirty, but you'd rather have leaders who don't *need* to get their hands dirty. Leadership is not about getting in the trenches with your employees, it's about making sure there are no obstacles to performance in those trenches.

Competence is in the ability to shift from a focus on processes to a focus on people: two completely different skillsets. Part of leading with a purpose is realizing that what brought you to where you are today is not necessarily going to keep you there or help you grow to where you want to be in the future. Great salespeople who move into leadership roles have to forego their technical skills in selling and client relationship management and embrace a new set of competencies, as a leader of other great salespeople.

This transition can be difficult for many because they are now not a team member, they are the leader of the team – the person that is going to influence the success of each individual and the organization. It involves a change in what they are valued for, what they are expected to deliver, and how they are rewarded. It can lead to a weakening of confidence if new competencies aren't developed.

Competence is being proficient in enabling your team so they have the space and freedom to do their job. It's helping them to make progress in their personal development. It's becoming practiced in supporting their schedules so they can get their work done. And it is acting as the buffer between the team and upper management.

Courage

Walt Disney once said, "Courage is the main quality of leadership, in our opinion, no matter where it is exercised. Usually it implies some risk—especially in new undertakings. Courage is to initiate something and to keep it going—to have a pioneering and adventurous spirit to blaze new ways in our land of opportunity."[8]

Courage is a powerful trait in leadership. It weaves together its Latin origin, *Cor*, meaning "heart," with its contemporary definition: mental or moral strength to venture, persevere, and withstand danger, fear, or difficulty. Courage is having the resolution and fortitude to change or stop something for the greater good. To us, the "heart" of courage is the substance of Leading *On Purpose*.

Winston Churchill represents a model of undeniable leadership with "world-changing" courage. When he spoke, England and its people were given the hope and determination to fight a war that simply had to be won – against odds that left many, even his own friends and family, convinced that England's future was already lost. [9]

Courage is a quality that separates good leaders from great ones. Leaders who demonstrate courage exude confidence and competence. They influence their people to act with bravery and drive organizational success. Human history is filled with iconic figures who exemplify the characteristics that define courageous leadership, such as resilience, commitment to purpose, and being authentic. Their passion, commitment, and resolve inspire their teams, energize customers, and position them as leaders in the markets they serve. For us, courage is foundational in that leaders need to step in front when something is challenging or difficult, or is simply not right.

Leading *On Purpose* takes courage. Risks taken may go against the grain of organizations, and key decisions can have game-changing effects on businesses. Given the consequences, there is often a reluctance for leaders to act with courage. We believe that hesitancy stems from a mindset that is results-based and not purpose-based.

The CEO of a four-billion-dollar company had to make a decision. The vice president of sales and marketing for North America had posted three straight years of 15+ percent growth year over year in both sales and profitability. The CEO loved this guy because of his performance. The numbers were great. However, customers, employees, and suppliers had little respect for this vice president because of the behaviors he was demonstrating.

What behaviors could possibly counter the accomplishments of this high-performing leader you ask? He was having multiple affairs with women in his organization. Problems started to bubble up and many others became aware of what was going on. The issue came to a head when an emotion-laden outburst at a sales meeting spurred words of anger between the vice president and two female colleagues.

Aware of the situation, the Human Resources leader completed an investigation and presented a comprehensive case to the division president and the CEO. She highlighted risks to the company such as loss of talent, employee engagement, customer anxiety, inequities in managing talent, difficulties in recruiting and retaining talent, and legal ramifications. It became immediately clear that any one of these risks alone could offset any gains in sales revenue and profitability. The HR leader recommended that the company let the vice president go.

The division president and CEO were reluctant at first. How could they fire the company superstar? They were looking forward to another double-digit year of growth. However, the HR leader was resilient and had the courage to engage the executives in a discussion of the risks, advantages, and potential outcomes. It took a little convincing, but the leaders finally agreed.

There are situations where you have to find the courage to do what's right for others and for the organization. How could one not take that action? To be fair, the division president and CEO found their courage as well.

Martin Luther King Jr. famously said, *"The ultimate measure of a man is not where he stands in moments of comfort, but where he stands at times of challenge and controversy."* Leaders will experience challenges throughout their careers; and some will be more complicated than others. How leaders manage through the difficult times defines whether others will follow. It will be uncomfortable, people may not like you, but they will respect you for having the courage to take a position, regardless of the political or business implications.

Curiosity

The phrase, "curiosity killed the cat" does not apply to leaders. In fact, curiosity is one of the cornerstones of great leaders. Agile Leaders are genuinely curious. They seek to ask questions and understand before they act or react. A curious mind is an agile mind, and the mindset of a curious leader opens with questions, not with answers. They pursue alternative points of view and encourage others to do the same.

When our curiosity is triggered, we assess perspective, we engage in deep discussion, and we think openly and rationally about decisions. The result is more creative solutions, shared accountability, and shared ownership of the decision. In addition, curiosity allows leaders to gain greater respect from others by continuously showing interest in what they have to say. A leader that seeks to understand and accept diverse options helps to inspire employees to form trusting and collaborative relationships with their colleagues.

Research has shown that when curiosity is activated, we are less likely to demonstrate Confirmation Bias[10] (looking for information that supports our beliefs rather than for evidence suggesting that we are wrong). We are also less likely to stereotype people (making broad judgments, such as that women or minorities don't make good leaders).

Curiosity is leading with questions, not answers. It's not your job as a leader to have all of the answers. If people come to you with a question, don't give them the answer and tell them what to do. Ask questions that help them to discover the answer themselves and understand more deeply, so they can make better decisions. People can't grow if you give them all the answers all the time. It discourages discovery and confidence building.

Curiosity is a quality of character in a leader that helps one grow in awareness and knowledge; it helps others grow by giving them voice; and it helps the organization grow and expand because of its ability to attract and retain talent with diverse perspectives.

As we stated at the onset of this chapter, our belief is that to be a leader who others truly want to follow, one must have a leadership mindset that is purpose-based, rather than results-based. They must lead for reasons that are greater than themselves.

While Chapter 1 defines what Leadership *On Purpose* is, sometimes the best way to sharpen the definition of something is to state its opposite. Chapter 2 presents you with what it isn't and demonstrates what attributes are missing in the mindset of leaders who are *Off* Purpose.

Reflection Questions

- Do you default to a Fixed or Growth Mindset? What actions will you take to build your comfort with a growth mindset?
- What do you do to help others not only see the story, but also write themselves into it?
- How can you increase the confidence people have in you?
- In what ways can you become more competent as a Leader *On Purpose*?
- Reflect on situations where you don't feel you influenced the result. How could you have been more courageous?
- Where and with whom do you need to be more curious? How will you do that?

2

LEADING *OFF* PURPOSE

Money motivates neither the best people, nor the best in people. It can move the body and influence the mind, but it cannot touch the heart or move the spirit; that is reserved for belief, principle, and morality.

—Dee Hock

In 2014, Wells Fargo was named the most valuable bank brand in the world according to the *Brand Finance 500* listing.[11] Since its founding over 160 years ago, its reputation had remained that of a reliable, trustworthy banking institution. Two years after receiving the recognition, Wells Fargo was fined $185 million by federal and California state regulators for widespread fraud involving 5,300 employees, all of whom were ultimately fired from the company. [12]

The scope of the scandal is stunning. The company lost billions of dollars, and worse, the trust and confidence of its customers. It's easy to imagine a few employees taking advantage of a company's systems, policies, or sales incentives for personal gain, but thousands committing fraud illustrates just how easy it is for so many people to be misled, or unled.

Research shows that people cheat more when they don't think they'll get caught or when they believe everybody else is doing it, which raises a series of important questions: where was the leadership over the course of the several years that this illegal behavior was happening; what were they doing to get in front of this at the onset; did they have the courage to stop it; and where was the accountability?

Anyone who's been in a leadership role knows that unauthorized and even illegal things can happen in an organization. Leaders *On Purpose* are always focused on the sustainability and success of others and the organization. They're swift to enact measures to protect people's jobs and their organization's reputation and success.

In Chapter 1, we shared what we believe it takes to be a leader who others truly want to follow, and to have a leadership mindset that is purpose-based. We shared how Leaders *On Purpose* are the kind who strive to have and maintain meaning in their careers and positively impact the growth and development of others. It's their growth mindset that welcomes others' ideas and is guided by the future impact of decisions and not the immediate results.

It is possible that a number of leaders at Wells Fargo knew that fraud was occurring, since it involved thousands of employees. Yet, over the course of several years, they didn't take measures to stop it. Maybe once discovered, they were hoping that the matter would resolve itself.

In Chapter 2, we'll explore how leadership can be *Off* Purpose. We'll identify the systems and behaviors that often derail organizations in their approach to identifying the right candidates to be leaders. It all begins with talented people ensuring they want to be leaders for the right reasons in the first place.

There are people who jump into leadership wanting to make a difference, but have little to no understanding of what leadership entails or fully comprehend the expectations of the job. A 10-year longitudinal study on executive leadership found that 50 to 60 percent of executives fail within the first 18 months of being promoted or hired into an executive position. Sixty-one percent of them said they were not prepared for the challenges once they accepted the position.[13]

Off Purpose leadership is as much a fault and ownership of the organization as it is of the individual – maybe more. When you consider the systems, policies, and selection criteria used by organizations to identify, assess, and choose its leaders, you realize that it's common practice for organizations to place people into leadership roles for the wrong reasons.

Based on over 40 years of research, the Gallup Report, *The State of the American Manager*, provides an in-depth look at what characterizes great managers. Their study of 2.5 million manager-led teams in 195 countries, measuring the engagement of 27 million employees, discovered that the majority of managers are *miscast* as leaders. According to Gallup's study, 82 percent of current managers do not have the leadership capabilities required for the role.[14]

Most organizations have seen this story played out time and time again. A high-performing individual contributor gets promoted for past technical performance and not for the leadership capability required in a future role. This individual may fail and many times is exited from the organization. What drives this behavior in organizations? What are the barriers created by organizations that lead to mistakes in identifying and developing emerging leadership talent? There are some common organizational behaviors that we think are a core cause of many talent management problems.

Seven Most Common Reasons Why People Are Promoted to Leadership

Organizations often rely on behavioral indicators to identify leadership potential in individuals, and that behavior becomes the sole or leading reason an individual is placed on a succession path. Below are seven of the most common criteria used by organizations to identify and select candidates as potential leaders. There are certainly more than the seven we've described here, but in our experience, these are of the most common. In a parallel sense, we consider these the *Seven Wrong Reasons for Promoting People into Leadership Positions*:

1. Past Performance

In our research, we have found that nearly 70 percent of organizations look at past performance as a predictor of future effectiveness, and make the mistake of not realizing that it's more than past achievements that define one's leadership ability. Perhaps it's a hope or even expectation for similar high-performance outcomes that compels organizations to select its leaders for this singular reason.

When you advance someone into a leadership position, they're likely not going to be involved in the same job they were involved in before. Their scope of involvement, type of activities, and level of responsibility change. The skills needed to be a leader are very different and cannot be taken for granted.

A high-performing engineer who achieves all of his metrics, designs great products, and is awarded a number of patents is promoted to chief of engineering and is now buried in meetings and budget discussions. As a result, the department begins to miss deadlines, milestones with clients, and quality metrics.

A sales specialist who's brilliant with prospects and clients and becomes known as "The Closer" for the company is promoted to director then vice president of sales and is now completely engaged with administrative work and personnel issues. Taking the best salesperson off the front lines ultimately caused the department to miss its sales quotas for the first time, and satisfaction scores among the largest clients begin to drop.

Many people vying for leadership roles often fail to realize that how they performed in the past has little relevance for them now in their new role as a leader of others and as someone responsible for encouraging and guiding the development and performance of others. They often become frozen in their mindset, thinking that they don't have to change. Because they've been promoted for their past performance, they often default to engaging in those activities that brought them success in the past, thereby creating a vacuum in leadership to the detriment of their team and that of the organization.

2. Relationship with Senior Management

The maxim, "It's about who you know" is one of the major reasons why people are selected and promoted into leadership positions. Embedded in this reasoning is the concession that becoming a leader is conditional upon knowing and being liked by people in senior management. We see this in a CEO candidate's relationship with the board of directors' chairperson of an organization or a mid-level leader's relationship with a senior executive two levels up. The senior executive mentors and advocates for the candidate as a successor to their position or as their nominee for a leadership role elsewhere in the organization based on the relationship, not on the long-term leadership capabilities.

People, knowing this standard, commit their time to marketing and positioning themselves in front of senior leaders in order to be seen as go-getters and leadership material. This can negatively influence candidates in many ways, including causing them to develop a sense of entitlement. Being a part of the "in-crowd," their expectation is that the job is theirs, setting their leadership careers *Off* Purpose from the start. They see their ideas, aspirations, and even agendas as more valid or important than other people's.

What's often neglected in all of this is the negative impact on other leadership candidates' levels of engagement and even retention, believing they were passed over because of a relationship and not assessed on the strength of their talents and skills.

We are not suggesting that it's wrong to develop strong connections with senior leadership. You're more effective as a professional and as a leader if you have enduring relationships and networks with people who can help advance your career and objectives.

Leaders *On Purpose* develop relationships with senior management and network for a higher purpose beyond that of their own personal goals or ambitions. Their relationships are authentic and become a means to a higher-purpose end for others and for their organizations.

3. Gregarious and a Good Self-Promoter

You have most likely heard the saying, "Empty vessels make the most noise?" It's a saying that means those with the least talent and knowledge often speak the loudest, frequently speak the most, and tend to make their presence felt the most – even though their capabilities may not be at the level required for a role. The bottom line is that the most outgoing, gregarious person who can promote themselves is a confident, enterprising person who wants to succeed and is perceived as having leadership capabilities in many organizations.

The Caliper Profile is a talent assessment tool that measures an individual's personality characteristics and motivations in order to predict on-the-job behaviors and future performance.[15]

This scientific instrument is one of a series of personality tools developed primarily to assist in the selection of candidates for a variety of different positions in an organization. It is very effective in identifying traits in talent that impact success in a role. The profile measures 22 traits that affect how a person is perceived by others. Their data shows that people who have different trait patterns can perform effectively in leadership roles more often because they are more visible and in front of the right people.[16]

When used holistically and compared with success profiles, this, and other similar instruments, help provide valid data for making decisions on selection, promotion, and development. However, taking into account specific traits independent of other data and making decisions based on those individual traits can lead to poor decisions when identifying leadership talent.

As an example, people given leadership positions because of their outgoing nature –people we often describe as "extroverts, assertive, and gregarious" – often fail because there may not be substance behind their sociability. The fact that they're able to speak convincingly and command conversations doesn't necessarily mean they'll be effective leaders. Some people who do well by this criterion may be self-promoters versus promoters of the organization or of their colleagues.

We have seen this many times in our work. When we reflect back on the organizations we've worked with across the industries and professions, the most common request from leaders wanting coaching for an individual was to help them improve their leadership presence – in their words – to be more outgoing, share and talk more, and be more assertive.

While these are all great characteristics of leaders, how they are demonstrated will differ. Organizations need to realize that a leader who is present, participates, and contributes may not always be the most outspoken, gregarious, aggressive person in the room. It often depends on the position, the organization, and its culture.

4. Hits a Home Run on a Big Project

Many have seen this story played out in their company. An individual does a great job on a highly-visible project, which is viewed by all as critical to the future of the organization.

Based on that person's performance and the success of that project, they're now on a succession path for a leadership role. This happens in multiple industries and professions, where a person's success in delivering impressively on a critical venture for the organization brands them as leadership material.

We personally managed a situation with a well-known high school teacher that every parent wants their child to have. Aside from being a great educator, Mary was also a great faculty member who was very personable, caring, and involved. She ultimately became the department chair and accepted the position knowing that it required her to coordinate the activities of three or four teachers once or twice a month. She didn't see the added responsibilities detracting from her classroom teaching and mentoring of students, the core of her interest and passion in education.

Mary performed so well as the department chair that the school board made her principal, where she then surprised everyone by failing miserably in her first year. She was no longer doing what she loved most, teaching children. Leading other teachers was not Mary's competency or purpose for being in education in the first place. She shortly stepped down as principal and went back to teaching full time.

The organization was *Off* Purpose in viewing her success as the department chair as an indication of leadership readiness or suitability. It could also be said that Mary was *Off* Purpose in accepting the role of principal, as she really wanted to teach. That was her purpose and passion. Even though she did this with the best intentions, Mary did not stay true to her purpose.

5. A Great Networker

People who interact well with others and know how to start and hold a conversation are considered to be great at networking. We believe networking is one of the most important behaviors for advancing one's career. Yet, organizations confuse a person's ability to interact with others for the purpose of developing professional or social contacts with having the mindset and capability for leadership.

Knowing the importance of networking to develop opportunities for advancement has encouraged many people to become very good at the practice. There are even social media platforms like LinkedIn purposefully designed to help facilitate making and sustaining connections. Certainly, many people are good at networking to begin with. They have great communication skills and know how to cultivate relationships with the right people.

It stands to reason that organizations would view a great networker more as leadership material than someone who projects shyness and awkwardness around others. But it doesn't always turn out that way.

Organizations keen on networking skills as a metric for leadership are evaluating people based primarily or solely on the networking skills and successes, and not on their intentions for making connections in the first place, which may often center on personal gain.

6. Reputable Degree vs. Life Experience

Organizations miss the mark when they select their leaders solely or primarily based on a college degree, the history and importance of the university they attended, or on the basis of advanced degrees or letters of certification. The assumption is that a degree indicates that a person is prepared and destined for leadership. Organizations fail to take into account the whole individual and their talents, experiences, capabilities, and aspirations – all those necessary elements that shape and prepare an individual for leadership.

A number of years ago, we worked with a young woman named Susan who grew up in South Africa. She got married, had two children, and was working toward completing her college degree when a difficult divorce upended her life, and in the process, compelled her and her infant daughters to move to the United States to start anew.

As a single, working mother, Susan managed to raise two incredibly smart and well-adjusted young women. She also worked hard to build a successful career at multiple global organizations. Although she was a few credits short of completing her baccalaureate degree from the University of South Africa, we hired her regardless into a senior director-level position.

When we assessed the whole individual, we realized that Susan was a person who had the courage and resilience to bring two young daughters to a country completely foreign to her, and with no acquaintances, find a job, work toward becoming a U.S. citizen, raise her daughters alone, and excel at her career. We really don't know many others who have experienced as many real-life crucibles, are more purpose-driven, and as a result, are more capable of leading others.

7. Reminds Me of Me

Hiring in one's own image is a trap into which leaders often fall. They identify someone who reminds them of themselves – whether in style, mannerisms, or appearances, and then focus their attention on that individual's training and development to ensure their success. Senior leaders tend to give their versions of themselves extra feedback and extra projects for greater exposure and experience.

Senior leaders often develop favorites, and then advocate for their pick to be either their successor or their nominee for a leadership position elsewhere in the organization. What they often neglect to take into consideration is whether that person has the capacity or even will to lead others and grow the organization.

In addition, when individuals know they're identified as favorites, they often conform to the senior leader's attitudes and parrot their behaviors, and end up assuming leadership roles without understanding or developing their own convictions and purposes for leading.

Senior leadership should allow individuals to develop their own unique identities and find their own strengths in leadership. The intent of the organization should be to develop effective, Agile Leaders who are willing themselves to seek out different points of view; who are not afraid to dissent in order to find a more effective and efficient solution.

Hiring in one's own image puts limitations on the new leader as well. That image becomes the only way the senior leader sees that individual. Moreover, it wrongly confers the same success the senior leader had in the past upon their person of choice, making the candidate seemingly infallible. In truth, hiring "someone who reminds me of me" often leads to low-change resiliency on the part of the new leader and an inability to adapt.

While they have all of the best of intentions, these seven most common reasons organizations select and promote people into leadership positions often become their seven most reoccurring mistakes. These criteria can become part of an organization's culture, thereby setting its leaders up for failure because the identification and selection criteria used are not quality criteria.

When organizations frame their succession thinking and decision-making around any of these seven criteria, new leaders will often fail for one of four common causes. To connect these causes to business outcomes, we will look at a couple of scenarios. Each reason is generally correlated to an absence of one of the *Four C's of Leading On Purpose*, as outlined in Chapter 1.

Scenario 1: Technical Competence vs. Leadership Competence

In this first, common scenario, the individual has all of the **competence** they need in their profession. They're very good at what they do, and because of their performance, they're viewed as having leadership potential. More times than not, their technical competence doesn't translate into leadership competence. By technical competence, we mean having the ability, knowledge, and skills to perform a task or process.

People with technical competence are often placed into leadership roles because of the results they are able to achieve. In leadership, however, people and strategic capabilities are needed much more than technical competence. When promoting someone based on their technical expertise, the results are often ineffective. Inventive, productive individual contributors become failed leaders and often end up leaving their organizations.

Scenario 2: Crowned the Leader Without Development or Support

How can an individual have *confidence* if they're brought into a position of leadership and responsibility over others and not given the development and support needed to be successful?

A recent study conducted by CareerBuilder of almost 4,000 U.S. employees revealed that 58 percent of managers hadn't received any form of management training; the majority, 57 percent, learned through trial and error.[17]

The harsh reality is that organizations are promoting people to positions of leadership who aren't trained in how to lead, inspire, and motivate others. This explains why 26 percent of these same managers admit that they weren't ready to become leaders when they took on the position and also why 50 to 60 percent fail within 18 months.[18]

Organizations often fail to commit the needed resources for training and development, especially as it pertains to mid-level leaders. They tend to do a better job of focusing resources on developing their senior leaders and onboarding and training new hires. Perhaps organizations assume those promoted from within are employees who already have first-hand knowledge of the company, and therefore will be able to transition quickly into their new roles and begin producing results. An all-to-often outcome is that the person promoted from within never fully integrates into their leadership role or develops an understanding of how best to write themselves into the story.

Scenario 3: Doing it for the Wrong Reasons

Perhaps the most unsettling outcome of organizations using the wrong criteria to identify leadership potential centers on the reasons why individuals pursue and accept leadership positions in the first place.

In the same study by CareerBuilder cited earlier, when U.S. employees were asked why they accepted a promotion, 50 percent of those surveyed said they became managers for "greater compensation," followed by another 39 percent who said they accepted the role in order to broaden their skills or seek some personal improvement.

Only 23 percent of those surveyed said they took a management role out of a desire to "lead others," while 21 percent said that "power and influence" was their reason for becoming a manager.[19] All in all, 70 percent were in it for either the compensation or for the power.

Additional studies have shown that money and power are poor motivators over the long-term. Those who accepted a leadership role for the money were 57 percent more likely to regret the promotion than those who wanted to make a greater contribution to their organization.[20]

There's a lack of **curiosity** in someone who goes into a leadership position for the money or power, or with the sole ambition to drive their own ideas forward, rather than having a real interest in what others could contribute to the success of an organization.

When you're an individual contributor, your curiosity rightly centers around you and what you need to learn and improve on. When you move into a leadership role, that mindset needs to shift. Your curiosity needs to center on what your people need in order to accomplish their jobs more effectively.

This insular thinking produces leaders with fixed versus growth mindsets, as we describe in Chapter 1, and is often focused on activities that ensure that their ideas succeed – regardless of the toll on others and on the organization.

Pat was relatively new in her leadership position and was pretty firm on what she believed needed to be done in her division. The organization hired her to drive her ideas forward. She, however, wasn't always interested in gaining support for her ideas. She seldom, if ever, had brainstorming sessions with her team or clients to broaden or modify her plans.

Pat didn't engage in meetings with clients to have a better idea of their needs firsthand and to find ways to improve the organization's products and services. She was always singularly focused on what she believed to be right and complete. As a result, Pat found it difficult to establish relationships and build momentum for her ideas.

We met Margaret while interviewing nurse managers about their role as managers of other nurses, what was important to them, and the kind of resources they needed in order to succeed in their positions. Margaret shared that she had been a nurse manager at a large hospital complex for the past two years, supervising a little over 100 nurses.

About 15 minutes into our conversation, she became emotional and teared up, revealing that she never really wanted to be a manager of nurses. Margaret loved serving and caring for patients. It's what she said gave her life and career meaning. But the leaders in the organization determined that she would be a good leader and strongly encouraged her to accept the nurse manager position. Although Margaret didn't want the job, she found it difficult to say no to better money and better hours. She did it because the organization convinced her to become a leader, yet they never gave her the necessary training or coaching on how to lead.

Both Pat and Margaret accepted their positions for the wrong reasons. Curiosity was not top of mind for either of them, which made it difficult for them to be successful in their roles.

Scenario 4: Expectations Differ

This last, yet very prevalent, scenario occurs when individuals don't clearly understand what's expected of them as leaders or have the *courage* to meet those expectations. It's an unsafe practice when organizations do not seek leaders who are going to step in front of issues and resolve them or lead an important change effort and instead promote individuals who hesitate, lose conviction for their ideas, or compromise their beliefs.

Leaders are often vulnerable to forces deterring them from standing up for what is right or just. They're often not willing to accept the repercussions for taking a stand, which could be a loss of office, title, or power. Individuals are often thrust into leadership positions for one or more of the seven reasons listed before, without understanding the expectations that come with that position.

Without conviction of thought and purpose, they're often fearful that senior management, their peers, or even their team members will disagree with and challenge them. They're reticent of others having a bad opinion of them or saying something negative about them because they took a stand on something that was controversial but nevertheless required leadership and doing. They were never trained and coached as leaders to have and show courage.

Being courageous isn't about being brazen enough to say anything and talk over others. That behavior is more tactless and inconsiderate than courageous. Sometimes it takes courage to wait for the right moment to speak or act.

In this chapter, we spoke of Leading *Off* Purpose, and while it's without question the responsibility of individuals to come into leadership for the right reasons, it's also incumbent upon organizations to identify, select, and encourage the right people for the right reasons.

The message for organizations is clear. Take a more holistic approach in identifying and selecting the right people who harbor the right reasons for wanting to lead. Make sure your candidates are clear on what's expected of them as leaders, and provide them with the tools, training, and support they need to help them grow and develop in their leadership.

Reflection Questions

- What were/are your reasons for going into leadership?
- As a leader, how do you look at and prioritize development of your team?
- Have you had an opportunity to make a decision that benefited others more than yourself? What did you do?
- How can you be more intentional about focusing on the impact you have on others?
- What are the barriers created by your organization that lead to mistakes in identifying and developing emerging leadership talent?
- Are you identifying talent based on future leadership capability or current technical performance?

3
THE SIX ATTRIBUTES OF
AN AGILE LEADER

Great leaders aren't necessarily smarter than the rest of us,
but they are more agile and mature.

—*Michael Holland*

The Myth

The old adage that culture originates at the top and filters down to touch and inspire every aspect of an organization has some flaws. Senior leaders have the least contact with and the slightest amount of influence over what people do every day and how people are directed and supported in an organization.

Setting the vision and demonstrating the behaviors are critical; however, senior leaders are often a very small and insular group of people supported by a small staff of direct reports. They typically have very little contact with the frontline workforce, and even less contact with customers. Their value and influence are found in setting the required levels of attainment and the expected behaviors of leaders and others in the organization. Top executives then enable the mid-level leaders to operationalize the strategy, anchor the behaviors, walk the talk, and inspire and engage others. In reality, the middle is where the magic happens and where organizations achieve the desired outcome ... culture!

In our assessment, mid-level leaders are the ones who touch virtually every aspect of an organization. They directly influence and, in many ways, define the culture. They encourage employees' sense of engagement, enhance the customer service experience, and ensure productive relationships with business partners and suppliers.

While senior leaders most importantly set the vision and define the direction and strategy for the organization, mid-level leaders take that strategy and bring it to life through the people and processes that make up the organization.

Mid-level leaders are a lot like the middle of an Oreo Cookie˚. The senior leadership team represents the top wafer of the cookie and the individual contributors right through to the customer-facing sales representatives comprise the bottom wafer.

What distinguishes an Oreo Cookie from any other cookie is its crème filling. If you remove the filling, you're left with just a couple of cookie wafers. The differentiator is the middle part that holds the whole thing together.

An organization clearly cannot operate without the top and bottom wafers, but the glue that keeps the wafers together, aligned, and 'on purpose' is the filling in the middle. Mid-level leaders connect with and help senior leadership in planning by offering feedback from all functional areas. They then directly communicate back down through the entirety of the bottom wafer on the strategy and support the execution right through to impacting the customer experience.

An example of the critical value of the two wafers and the middle filling can be found in running a hospital. To be an effective, trusted, and dependable medical center requires skilled and visionary administrators who manage the institution, set the market direction, secure the funding, and ensure the provisioning of the medical services the community requires.

Trust and dependability also require the presence and practice of quality health care professionals providing best-in-class services to their patients – from accurate diagnoses of medical conditions and diseases, to the most advanced treatments, bedside care, and responsiveness.

Administrators and clinicians are undoubtedly critical pieces for the successful functioning of a hospital, but both pieces cannot operate independent of each other. They each need the middle filling to deliver on the medical center's promise of safe and dependable healthcare and to operate the campus effectively and efficiently every hour of every day.

Mid-level leaders touch all areas of a hospital, including operations and equipment, physicians, health information technicians, nursing, medical records, billing, and more. They analyze and report on the effectiveness of each department and work with administrators and clinicians alike to attain the hospital's financial goals, maintain budgets, and most importantly, ensure the uninterrupted delivery of quality healthcare.

Leaders *On Purpose* who want their organizations to succeed recognize that mid-level leaders need to be identified, selected, developed, trusted with authority, and supported with resources. These leaders influence their organizations to become employers of choice to attract top talent, then train and develop that talent to help shape and execute strategy, engage employees, provide a great customer experience, and continuously adapt the organization to a dynamic marketplace.

A Focus on the Middle Majority

The greatest percentage of leaders in any organization of substantial size is typically found in the middle. Yet, organizations habitually fall short when it comes to committing resources for the training and development of this middle majority. They often do a better job in developing and supporting senior leaders and new hires. This is affirmed by the studies we shared in Chapter 2 revealing that 58 percent of managers hadn't received any form of management training, and that more than half fail in their role within the first 18 months.[21]

Mid-level leaders are critical to an organization's sustainability and success. Yet, to be effective as leaders in the middle, they need to possess the attributes and demonstrate the behaviors that will help them influence both up and down the organization.

Many organizations have leadership competency models that encompass anywhere from 10 to 30 behaviors that every leader must demonstrate to be successful. We feel that that's far too many. It's virtually impossible for individuals to understand, develop, and master all of those behaviors. Nevertheless, there are specific attributes that we believe are of utmost importance and can be remembered and mastered.

In our research on the effectiveness of leaders in global and domestic organizations, we have identified six attributes that are consistently present in successful leaders. For mid-level leaders to succeed as the middle filling capable of binding and aligning the entire organization, developing and applying skills and behaviors around these six attributes is imperative.

Our *Six Attributes of Agile Leaders* are the main ingredients in our recipe for mid-level leaders who are capable of taking the goals of senior leaders and the desires of individual contributors and tying and advancing them together for the sustainability and success of the organization. Before we introduce the six attributes, we want to share our perception of Agile Leadership, for it is the foundational mindset from which these attributes are able to take root and develop.

Agile Leaders are effective change agents who foster collaboration, build high-performing teams, and drive consistent results. They are found to have deep personal integrity and a willingness to learn from experience, and translate that knowledge into action. They're resilient and maintain positive outlooks during the inevitable changes that occur in life and business.

They view organizations holistically and demonstrate a natural aptitude to coach others and develop relationships built on guidance, trust, and inspiration. This type of leadership has a direct effect on employee engagement, which directly impacts innovation, productivity, and the financial performance of the organization, regardless of the industry.

Agile Leadership

When we thought about Agile Leadership and people with adaptive minds, Mike was reminded of someone he worked with in the retail industry 20 years ago, at the onset of the Internet Age. At the time, retail was primarily brick and mortar, and Chris, an executive in sales and marketing for Jockey Inc. for 25 years, knew the business well. Additionally, he had worked for many of the big retail companies earlier in his career.

Jockey was already one of the most recognized brands in the world, and much of the company's success could be attributed to Chris' ideas and marketing strategies. The company was able to make dramatic and timely shifts and expand its distribution channels. Outlet malls were just beginning to populate the national landscape, and Chris was on the leading edge of that change, moving the company from distributing solely through retailers such as Macy's and J.C. Penny's to owning its own outlet stores.

At the same time, Chris was guiding the company in the launch of its first eCommerce site, when many companies were just starting to look into eCommerce. Many were avoiding confronting the change altogether or waiting for others to do it first. Many feared Internet sales would simply cannibalize sales from retail stores and outlet malls.

Chris, on the other hand, typified an agile mind and Leadership *On Purpose*. Since the 1990s, new technologies, new competitors, and changing economies have brought significant shifts to the entire retail industry, requiring truly adaptive leadership, and Chris was there every step of the way – and was often a step ahead.

Agile Leaders are people who have a willingness to learn from experience and translate that knowledge into action. Their growth mindset keeps them resilient during the unforeseen yet inevitable changes that arise in life and in business.

Moreover, Agile Leaders demonstrate genuine curiosity and transparency when dealing with others, and in our experience, are often found leading the most innovative, productive teams. Their talent in asking questions in order to understand – and genuinely listening to alternative points of view – draws in and engages employees and makes them truly believe that their ideas count, which allows them to write themselves into the story.

The Gallup study we cited in Chapter 2, reporting on 2.5 million manager-led teams, had measured the engagement scores of 27 million employees and discovered that the following qualities that make great managers exist in only about one in ten people.[22]

- They motivate their employees,
- They assert themselves to overcome obstacles,
- They create a culture of accountability,
- They build trusting relationships, and
- They make informed, unbiased decisions for the good of their team and company.

The same report also found that companies that hire managers based on these talents see a 48 percent increase in profitability, a 22-percent increase in productivity, and a 19-percent decrease in turnover.[23]

Agile Leaders are rare though, and companies often have a hard time determining who does and doesn't have what it takes to be an adaptive, inspiring, and engaging leader. In our practice, we've identified *The Six Attributes of Agile Leaders* that we will introduce together here and explore in-depth individually in the chapters that follow.

The Six Attributes of Agile Leaders

Personal Integrity

Most people would like to believe that they have integrity, that they're honest, principled, and live life by a code of ethics. And we agree. Most of us work hard at leading upright lives. To us, Personal Integrity is more about your presence as a leader and how you practice strong and solid principles of effective leadership.

To us, Personal Integrity is exhibiting as a matter of habit, honest and truthful actions sourcing from honest and truthful intentions, a congruence between intention and behavior. Leaders *On Purpose* lead with this attribute. It is also about making and meeting your commitments while following the "Platinum Rule: Do unto others as they would like done unto them." Finally, it includes establishing leadership presence and principles, including personal brand, ethics, trust, and transparency. It also means that a leader makes and meets their commitments.

While Personal Integrity may not require a particular skill or talent, Agile Leaders understand the importance in being consistent in their nature and standards, in demonstrating ethical resolve in every instance, and in openly communicating with others and on a timely basis. These are the primary qualities that comprise Personal Integrity and gain the loyalty and trust of employees and others.

Learning Agility

Being learning agile not only positively affects one's personal success, but it can also positively impact others. John Maxwell recognized this in his book, *21 Irrefutable Laws of Leadership*. Law #1: The Law of the Lid: Your team will never exceed the capacity of the leader."[24]

Learning Agility involves the ability and willingness to learn from experience and then apply that learning to perform successfully in new situations. Research from the Center for Creative Leadership has determined that a major difference between successful people and those whose careers falter is their ability to translate meaning from their experiences into changes in behavior.[25]

Experience matters, regardless of whether you are a natural leader or someone who has learned to be an effective leader. Experience is where you gain the lessons learned that help you to determine where and how to change your behavior.

The most valuable experiences push you out of your comfort zone, stretch your skills, and challenge your abilities. Though nobody wants to spend their entire career in a constant state of discomfort, the most worthwhile leadership development usually comes with a dose of it.

Research by the Korn Ferry Institute indicates just how vital Learning Agility is to successful leaders – potentially more impactful than EI, IQ, or one's educational background. Leaders with high Learning Agility are identified as top potential leaders 18 times more often than those with low Learning Agility. And senior executives demonstrating Learning Agility are viewed as five times more engaged and promoted twice as fast.[26]

If you want to grow your team and your success as a leader, you need to keep learning and growing personally. If you limit yourself to thinking you can relax and stop acquiring new knowledge because you have the title and influence, you're actually putting a lid on the team's ingenuity and capability. You're sentencing them to never exceed your capability.

Coaching Others

The ultimate mindset for leaders isn't how far they advance themselves, but how far they advance others in the organization. The focus of an Agile Leader should always be on the growth and development of others. Agile Leaders accept accountability for the active development of their team members. They not only empower others to act, but also remove the obstacles to their success. We believe that the greatest compliment a leader can receive is to have other people want to hire members of their team. Coaching Others enables employees to grow and achieve their potential, utilize their talents, and make an even greater contribution to the organization.

Coaching Others is also having the courage to engage in critical and uncomfortable conversations with team members so they may have an opportunity to grow and change. If you fail to be honest and forthright for fear of hurting someone's feelings, there's a chance that you're going to hurt them professionally and hurt your brand as a leader in the organization.

When we talk about Coaching Others, we're talking about more than coaching. We're talking about how to provide feedback to others, how to mentor others, and how to delegate to others. We're encouraging ongoing conversations for the development of the people you work with, while keeping in mind your own development.

Agile Leaders are able to move their organizations forward because they have the ability to identify and cultivate talent within their teams. They accomplish this by engaging their people, by including them in planning and decision-making, by holding them accountable, and by developing and improving their capabilities.

Followership

When we think of Followership, Sir William Wallace comes to mind as portrayed by Mel Gibson in the film, "Braveheart." Wallace was a Scottish knight who became a leader during the First War of Scottish Independence in the 1300s and inspired the Scots to fight to the death for their country's freedom, which they eventually won.

There are many facets to Followership that we'll share in more detail in Chapter 7. But to summarize here: it's about your ability to inspire, to build relationships, and to build your credibility with others so that people will trust and follow you.

Followership is about your ability to create followers, and it's also about you having the humility to admit when you don't know something. It's having the humbleness to step aside and let someone else take the lead when it's appropriate. It doesn't mean you're less of a leader, it means that you're letting someone with greater talent take the lead.

A leader's ability to step aside enables others to get involved and engaged in the process, which in itself builds Followership.

When we worked together at Aurora Health Care, Mike would often take the work of the team forward and present it to senior leadership. He knew when it was best for him, as the department head, to take certain issues forward.

There were many times that Mike would encourage individual team members to meet with senior leaders. He knew that his people worked long hours on a project or were the subject matter experts on an issue, so he wanted them to have the face time in order to grow and be recognized for their work. Because of the trust between Mike and his team, they easily exchanged the role of leader and follower when appropriate.

Some people will never believe in themselves until someone else does. Part of an Agile Leader's role is to help others grow by being the *confidence catalyst* and stepping aside so that others may shine.

Systems Thinking

The best leaders are seen as acting in the best interests of the organization as a whole. Viewing the organization from a broad perspective, what we describe as Systems Thinking, includes seeing the overall structures, patterns, and cycles, rather than only specific functions or events.

Agile Leaders understand how things influence one another within a whole, and in this fashion, view the organization as an ecosystem. With this mindset, Agile Leaders maintain a finger on the pulse of things occurring in an organization, knowing that activities, interventions, or changes in one area can have an effect in other areas, and even on the organization as a whole.

This comprehensive approach helps leaders to quickly identify the real causes of problems and know exactly where to work to address them. In other words, understanding the system means leaders can navigate more easily and know what kind of support will be necessary for important initiatives.

To establish Systems Thinking, Agile Leaders break down silos and build networks with individuals from all corners of the organization in order to help identify issues and opportunities from different perspectives.

Employees, when introduced to this mindset, feel empowered and like a part of something larger than themselves. When they can understand their purpose and work effort in the context of the organization as a whole, they begin to write themselves into the story.

Change Resiliency

Change Resiliency is effectively leading yourself and others through the inevitable changes faced by an organization. It means being able to maintain consistent personal integrity and a level of productivity through a variety of situations.

Leaders with Change Resiliency are the ones who "make it look easy" when everyone else seems overwhelmed. Leading gracefully through change can seem impossible at times, but the problems associated with change are generally not because of the change itself, but because of the – sometimes challenging – transitions that are required.

When faced with change, Agile Leaders embrace it. They'll take the lead and provide context around the purpose of the change or cause of the disruption and define expected behaviors. They focus on the benefits of change and strive to create stronger buy-in and alignment from others.

Agile Leaders show genuine interest and actively listen. They demonstrate empathy and patience in order to help people transition at their own pace, while also encouraging and nudging people to step outside of their comfort zones.

Change Resiliency comes down to what leaders do to prepare to lead themselves and others through change. If they're focused too much on process and not enough on people, the negative consequences can be fairly significant. There are many stories of companies that have acquired other companies and simply forced their processes, procedures, and policies into the company being acquired.

The brutal fact is that 70 percent of change initiatives fail. Whether you follow McKinsey, Gallup, Harvard Business Review, or other institutions and their research, this huge percentage is often referenced. We have found that most organizations experience four to five significant changes every year, so the key questions have to be:

- "Why do change efforts fail in organizations?"
- "Why aren't companies ready for or resilient to change?"

In most of the studies and research completed, there appear to be two symptoms that consistently show up when asking the question, "WHY?" – lacking a clear vision and removing obstacles to that clear vision. Where do these miscalculations come from? What is the core cause to these symptoms of the problem you ask? Leaders … full stop.

We often talk ourselves into or out of things. For example, consider how many times people have sworn that they're going to lose weight, yet they still find themselves locked in the same dilemma time and again: *"Do I order the cheeseburger or do I order the tuna salad?"*

Our minds are telling us to order the tuna salad, and yet we order the cheeseburger, with bacon, because it's difficult to push away the things that we need to push away.

> *We talk ourselves into being change resistant far more*
> *often than we talk ourselves into being change resilient.*

Leaders with a mindset that's change resistant will often find someone or something to blame when things go awry or fail. They'll blame upper management, or blame departments that failed to deliver materials on time, or blame suppliers, or even blame the stockholders. Yet as an Agile Leader, whether you agree with the change or not, you realize that placing blame is not acceptable or productive. Your job is to drive the change forward.

As we stated earlier, exceptional managers are rare, though we believe *The Six Attributes of Agile Leaders* can help organizations determine who has the ability and agility to be a Leader *On Purpose*.

In Chapter 4, we'll begin our deep dive into the six attributes by leading off with the attribute of Personal Integrity and the mindset and behaviors that comprise that characteristic. With it, Agile Leaders lead more meaningful lives, and are true to themselves, true to others, and true to the organization.

Reflection Questions

- Where do you see yourself with regard to these Six Agile Leadership Attributes?
- What are areas of personal develop that you are focused on and how do they connect to these six attributes?
- Think of successful leaders you have worked with – which of these six attributes did they demonstrate?
- What are some of the behaviors that leaders show on a daily basis that directly relate to these six agile leadership attributes?
- What is one attribute you feel you can focus on and develop as part of your personal development plan?

4
PERSONAL INTEGRITY

It really is simple, great leaders make and meet their commitments.

—*Rachel Kohler*

For four generations, the Kohler family has built and advanced one of America's oldest and most successful privately-held companies. The Kohler Company, best known for its plumbing products, and more recently known for its furniture, cabinetry, tile, engines, and generators, is ranked by *Fortune* among the Top 25 most important U.S. private companies.[27]

Rachel Kohler, is the great granddaughter of founder John Michael Kohler, and during Mike's time at Kohler, was Group President of the Interiors Business. Rachel is a leader who is deeply focused on identifying and developing talent, and she would often discuss the behaviors that were of utmost importance for real leaders to possess – behaviors that build trust and integrity and explain the 150 years of Kohler success.

- Feedback is a gift: accept it, positive or negative. You gain respect by listening.
- If you want to build trust and integrity with your teams and others, you have to actually *build it*. You have to make commitments and meet commitments consistently.

These two behaviors resonated the most with Mike as foundational in building Personal Integrity in an Agile Leader.

Change in Your Pocket

An analogy we like to use about building trust and integrity is having change in your pocket. Every time you do something that builds trust or helps people align with you, you collect change in your pocket. It could be a quarter here or a dime there for your promises made and kept.

You want to build continuously the amount of change you have, for there will be times, but hopefully not often, where you'll have to give back some of that change for missing a commitment or some other deficit. The key is making sure that you've built enough integrity and credibility so that when you make those mistakes, people will understand. Everyone makes mistakes. Your goal is to make them rare. To always have change in your pocket.

Many leaders make mistakes without establishing a level of integrity and credibility. Many feel they don't have to establish their persona in the eyes of others. They view themselves as the most senior person in the room, and therefore don't require feedback or feel a need to explain themselves.

Rachel Kohler shared what she believed are the enduring qualities of leadership, but there are many other characteristics and behaviors that compose Personal Integrity.

John Maxwell once said, "The respect that leadership must have requires that one's ethics be without question. A leader not only stays above the line between right and wrong, he stays well clear of the gray areas."

In Warren Buffet's words, "In looking for people to hire, look for three qualities: integrity, intelligence, and energy. And if they don't have the first one, the other two will kill you."

Personal Integrity is the first attribute we focus on when defining an Agile Leader. A leader's integrity is often based on one's leadership presence and the principles followed. We believe one's personal brand, trustworthiness, ethical resolve, and communication and transparency are key to being viewed as a leader with Personal Integrity.

Booher Research surveyed over 200 professionals in a variety of industries to ask them their reasons for wanting to increase their personal presence. Forty-eight percent said their reason was either to increase their credibility or sell their ideas and projects. According to Booher, that percent of respondents hasn't changed over the past 30 years.[28]

Additionally, when participants were asked, "In general, how much does someone's personal presence affect how much credibility they have with you?" almost 75 percent replied, "A great deal."[29]

Agile Leaders convey their unique presence through their values. They make and meet commitments while demonstrating ethical resolve in every circumstance. It is the primary quality that gains the loyalty and trust of employees. They act with resilience and determination even when decisions may not be popular. They demonstrate genuine curiosity, active listening, and transparency when engaging with others by quieting their inner voice, focusing on the person, asking good open-ended questions, and listening in order to understand.

We believe Agile Leaders lead with integrity through their personal brand, their trustworthiness, their ethical resolve, and their communication and transparency. But what exactly does 'leading with integrity' look like? It's actually a combination of many behaviors and practices, including:

- Leading by example and being a role model to others. This defines your personal brand and presence in the eyes of others.
- Consistently being honest and trustworthy in all of your actions.
- Following through on commitments and doing the right thing.
- Demonstrating ethical resolve.
- Communicating with intention and transparency in all situations and in all formats, whether spoken or written.

Agile Leaders realize that their Personal Integrity – as reflected by their words, actions, decisions, and methodologies – helps to create their organizations' true values and culture. Studies show that this attribute extends benefits to both leaders and their organization.

- Research has linked greater integrity with increased workplace performance.[30]
- Leaders with integrity foster greater trust and satisfaction from their direct reports, who are then more likely to follow suit.[31]
- Employees serving under high-integrity leaders demonstrate more positive workplace behaviors (e.g., helping others during busy periods) and fewer negative workplace behaviors (e.g., falsely calling in sick).[32]
- Employees who trust their leaders to have integrity are likely to work harder, perform better, and have greater company loyalty.[33]

We have developed a simple self-assessment to help you identify your strengths and gaps. How often do you lead with Personal Integrity? What are you known for as a leader? Take a moment to complete this self-assessment to measure how often you lead with integrity. Before answering each statement, reflect on your recent actions and decisions and on your presence as a leader.

How Often Do You Lead with Integrity?
Self-Assessment

Behavior	5 = Almost Always 1 = Seldom
I meet the deadlines and commitments that I make to others.	
I tell the truth when it may make me look bad.	
I admit when I make mistakes.	
I pause to think about the impact of my decisions before I make them.	
I act and talk the same way when I am around people as when I am not.	
I avoid engaging in conversations about others when they're not present.	
I am curious about understanding people and their perspectives.	
I provide direct feedback to people, rather than talking poorly about them behind their back.	
I act in consistent ways.	
Total	

A score of 35 or better indicates that you work hard at leading with integrity, while scores below 35 suggest that you may be deficient in one or more of the core elements of Personal Integrity: Personal Brand, Trust, Ethical Resolve, and Communication and Transparency. Let's explore the dynamics of these core elements.

Personal Brand

Personal Brand is defined as how you are known and how you are described by others. Your brand is anything about you that will create an image or impression in the minds of those you interact with. This includes:

- Your name and how you use your title.
- Your tone of voice and non-verbal communication.
- Your reputation as a person and professional, including the confidence people have in you and how competent you are in your area of responsibility.
- Your presence and how you hold yourself.

- The way you dress.

Establishing your brand is an ongoing process as words, actions, and appearances can have both a positive and negative impact on your presence in the eyes of others.

Trust

Trust is the degree to which you are honest with others and can be trusted by others. It's also established by the amount of belief you place in others. How do leaders build a reputation for high levels of trust? They demonstrate the behavior and then their story transcends throughout the organization.

We believe storytelling is one of the most powerful ways to promote examples of leaders trusting in others. These stories highlight what people did that was successful and earned that trust. The integrity of an organization stems from how leaders behave and how they bring that attribute to life through trust.

The Ritz-Carlton Hotel Company has 20 values that comprise what is referred to as "The Ritz-Carlton Basics." Each day, in a brief session called the "Daily Lineup," supervisors review one of the 20 values with their staff, and each Monday, all Ritz-Carlton Hotels world-wide celebrate an example of a staff member who went beyond the call of duty to live up to one of the 20 Ritz-Carlton Basics.

These practices help maintain a high level of organizational integrity because employees know the Ritz-Carton's values and are more likely to apply them. The Ritz-Carlton's integrity has contributed to the organization receiving all of the major awards bestowed by the hospitality industry and leading consumer organizations.

People determine how trustworthy a leader is based on their capability, transparency, and integrity. They demonstrate a positive level of vulnerability with leaders they trust, and are more inclined to be satisfied with and loyal to them. The link between integrity and trust cannot be overestimated in the relationship leaders have with their company's employees or with their country's citizens.

Dwight D. Eisenhower was an inspiring and effective leader who became a five-star general in the United States Army during World War II, and served as Supreme Commander of the Allied Expeditionary Force in Europe. Following the war, he became the 34th president of the United States for the purpose of protecting what he had defended.[34] The one word that practically all of his superiors and subordinates alike used to describe President Eisenhower was trust. He was trustworthy, for he believed it to be a cornerstone of integrity. As he stated,

"The supreme quality for leadership is unquestionably integrity. Without it, no real success is possible, whether it is on a section gang, a football field, in an army, or in an office."

Leaders understand the stakes of not having the trust of their people or not placing trust in their people. Pricewaterhouse Cooper's 2016 Global CEO Survey reported that 55 percent of CEOs believe that a lack of trust is a threat to their organization's growth.[35]

But most have done little to increase trust in their organizations; in fact, just the opposite. In 2013, 37 percent of CEOs saw lack of trust as a threat.[36]

Compared with people at low-trust companies, people at high-trust companies report:[37]

- 74% less stress
- 106% more energy at work
- 50% higher productivity
- 13% fewer sick days
- 76% more engagement
- 29% more satisfaction with their lives
- 40% less burnout

Following the success of Google's Project Oxygen research which studied what makes a great manager, Google researchers applied a similar methodology to discover the "secrets of effective teams." Much of the work done at Google, and in many organizations now, is done collaboratively by teams.

The goal was to answer the question: "What makes a team effective at Google?" New research reveals surprising truths about why some work groups thrive and others falter. According to their study, the number one characteristic of the most effective teams is "trust."[38]

If you want people to push the envelope and come up with fresh creative approaches to business challenges, they can't be afraid to share their ideas.

Ethical Resolve

Ann Mulcahy, former CEO of Xerox Corporation, had a reputation for being candid. Shortly after becoming CEO, she announced that Xerox's business model was unsustainable and that the company would confront reality and then make the tough decisions necessary to restore Xerox's competitiveness. One employee told the press,

"Part of her DNA is to tell you the good, the bad, and the ugly."

Because of her integrity, Ann Mulcahy gained the trust of Xerox employees. They pulled together, gave their best efforts, and returned Xerox to profitability. One Xerox board member described the turnaround as a "minor miracle."

Ethics is acting in ways consistent with what society and individuals typically think are good values. Ethics is knowing right from wrong and leading with moral principles. It's acting in ways that are consistent with what people and society as a whole largely believe are the right values to lead and live by. These include:

- Respect for others and leading inclusively
- Standards of behavior
- Honesty
- Objectivity

At the boom of the computer industry in the 1990s, Mark Faris's company, Interlink Communications, entered into a business partnership with Cisco Systems to sell refurbished equipment. Business was booming for Interlink, but crashed in the 2000s. At one point in their partnership, Cisco began to pressure Interlink to drop or deemphasize its used equipment offerings.

When Interlink declined, Cisco discouraged customers from working with Interlink, resulting in a 30-percent loss of top-line revenues. Upset by Cisco's treatment of its partner, Faris began reselling replacement parts from Cisco as new parts at a profit, defrauding Cisco of $490,000.[39]

Initially, Faris fought the charges against him, but after talking with his family and friends, he recognized his own arrogance and greed and pled guilty. Faris spent nine traumatic months in prison, where less than ten percent of the inmates were white collar felons.

Being a convicted felon, he had difficulty resuming a professional career. Instead, he started public speaking and training to educate others about avoiding the unethical path he had taken. Faris is now using his experience to teach students and businesspeople that "if it can happen to me, it can happen to them."[40]

Communication and Transparency

Communication and Transparency include communicating appropriately for the audience, ensuring understanding, and being transparent with what you know.

This doesn't mean that every idea should be simply accepted, so as not to offend anyone. Creative discussions should be honest and critical, yet open-minded and respectful of other perspectives. Telling someone their bad idea is great and then ditching it on the quiet is hardly a sign of integrity.

Create a culture where people are encouraged to speak freely and share ideas. At the same time, teach them how to give and receive constructive feedback in a way that will develop and improve more ideas.

Every leader in every organization will generally state that they are 'pro-integrity.' But do they truly know what integrity actually means and can they clearly communicate that to each employee?

Do their actions speak louder than their words? Do leaders translate their definition into specific behavioral expectations? Leaders need to model and then actively and visibly reinforce integrity for everyone in the organization; this is true for the executive team as well as leaders at every level of the organization.

Shadow of a Leader

After Goodyear Tire lost money in 1990 (for the first time in 60 years), the board persuaded Stan Gault, a Goodyear Director and former CEO of Rubbermaid, to come out of retirement and replace Goodyear's current CEO. When Gault arrived, he began to unplug lights and unscrew light bulbs in the former CEO's large office, to reduce costs. He ate in the company cafeteria with the rest of the employees and got rid of executive parking spaces.

The word spread like wildfire among Goodyear employees that Gault believed "thrift is a virtue." When Gault then asked all Goodyear employees to help reduce the company's bloated costs, they already knew that their leader walked the talk. Goodyear employees responded to Gault's integrity and his plea to reduce costs. As a result, the company paid down its debt and invested in new research and development. Soon thereafter, Goodyear launched the newly developed "Aquatred Tire®." It was a huge success and Goodyear was restored to profitability.

As leaders, we all have a shadow that we cast over others in the organization that is either positive or negative and is both ahead of us and behind us. What is our shadow saying about us before we actually get there, or what is our shadow saying behind us, after we leave?

Organizations that flounder because of ethical issues usually indicates that there are leaders in that organization who are not ethical, and that negative shadow casts over others. Alternately, leaders *On Purpose* cast a positive shadow – as Stan Gault did for Goodyear – and help their organizations succeed and flourish.

A leader's shadow can also strengthen a company's culture and the engagement and commitment of its employees. In March of 2020, when retail outlets were initially forced to close their doors because of the COVID-19 pandemic, Tim Boyle, president and CEO of Columbia Sportwear Company, cut his salary to $10,000 a year, while Columbia retail employees still received their regular pay. His pay cut helped to keep almost 3,500 retail employees compensated during that time of uncertainty. In addition to Boyle's own pay cut, 10 top executives each voluntarily took a 15-percent pay reduction.[41]

That's a shadow of a leader. In this example, it's someone who acts – someone who talks about the values and then lives those values. With that mindset, they gain the respect of others; even those who disagree will hold them in higher esteem for their convictions.

As the following diagram shows, our leadership shadow can be defined through using four different personas. These characters are formed by how much leaders *"Talk the Talk"* and *"Walk the Talk."* How much do leaders talk about what needs to be done or about the desired behaviors that need to be shown, and how much do they lead by example by exhibiting the behaviors they expect others to display?

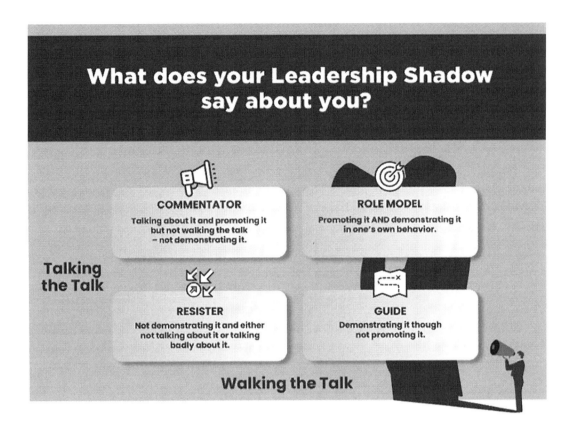

What does your Leadership Shadow say about you?

COMMENTATOR
Talking about it and promoting it but not walking the talk – not demonstrating it.

ROLE MODEL
Promoting it AND demonstrating it in one's own behavior.

Talking the Talk

RESISTER
Not demonstrating it and either not talking about it or talking badly about it.

GUIDE
Demonstrating it though not promoting it.

Walking the Talk

<u>*The Commentator*</u> is the leadership shadow that does a lot of talking about how people should act and what people should do, but their actions do not align with what they're saying. This could be because they don't understand what they are commenting on or perhaps because they think that because they're a leader, it doesn't apply to them. This is probably one of the worst shadows a leader could cast.

Lisa's *Commentator Shadow* could be seen recently. She attended a meeting with her peers in order to share the recent survey information about how the new leadership behaviors were settling within the organization, one of which was "Openness to others' thoughts and ideas." When the data she presented was challenged by a colleague, she got very angry and started to argue with the person and tell them how wrong they were.

Commentators are people who are skilled at talking about what should be done or how others should behave, but they're not putting it into practice themselves. Are you a do as I say, not as I do leader, or someone who talks about what's right and then lives it and demonstrates it in your leadership?

<u>*The Resister*</u> is a leader who is not demonstrating the desired behaviors, actions, or values

expected of leadership, and either talking badly to others about those expected behaviors, actions, or values, or not talking about them at all.

Paul's *Resister Shadow* appeared during a lunch meeting with his team. They were discussing the tight timelines they had been given for a new project. As Paul was walking away from the table, he said,

"I don't really care what they say, I will get it done when I get it done."

The Guide is a leader who demonstrates the desired behaviors or actions, but isn't very vocal about those expectations. This may be because they are uncomfortable talking about it or because they simply don't think about talking about it.

Max has a *Guide Shadow* that shows in almost everything he does. He is an effective leader, but is very quiet about his leadership. You don't always know what he is thinking because he doesn't share much. When you watch him lead his team or interact with his peers, though, he is a walking model of the leadership behaviors that the company expects. You would be hard pressed to find anything Max does that doesn't align with the image expected of leaders within his organization.

The Role Model is essentially the shadow of leaders who practice what they preach. *The Role Model* talks positively about what is expected of leaders within their organizations and makes sure that their behaviors, actions, and presence demonstrate those expectations.

Jenny leads *On Purpose*. She strongly believes in, supports, and demonstrates the new leadership expectations that the organization has rolled out. Her *Role Model Shadow* prompts her to share feedback with others and encourage them to also be role models so that the organization will truly set itself apart from their competitors and help win the war for talent in their industry.

She coaches others so they understand how they can better align their behavior and actions to those expectations, and when planned or unplanned, you can always see Jenny demonstrating and putting into practice everything she is explaining to and expecting from others.

One example of this was after a very busy week at the office. Jenny was really behind with her emails and wanted to work on getting caught up over the weekend. The organization, however, had just asked everyone to be respectful of other's time away from the office and not send emails after business hours or on the weekends.

Earlier that year, she had told her team that just because she sends emails out on the weekends, in no way did she want or expect them to respond to them. After much thought, Jenny decided that rather than sending emails out over the weekend, she would prioritize how she would respond to them on Monday.

Leading with integrity is about the behaviors you demonstrate, the impact you have on others, and the choices you make. It's about pausing long enough to consider the choices available to you and then making or responding in a way that aligns with what you want to accomplish. It is about staying true to your values and assessing all relevant information before you commit to a decision.

Making Better Choices

In May of 2005, professional tennis player Fernando Verdasco of Spain was serving to America's top player, Andy Roddick, at the Rome Masters in Milan, Italy. Verdasco had lost the first set and was down 5-3, love-40, triple match point. He hit deep on the second serve. The line judge called the ball out and Roddick had the match, only Roddick refused to accept the point. Verdasco's serve had nicked the line, he said. Stunned, the umpire let Roddick overrule him. Verdasco then fought back, held serve, and won the set and then the match.[42]

Unless you're a tennis enthusiast, you most likely never heard about this extraordinary display of generosity. It barely rated a mention in the American press. Yet, Roddick risked and lost tens of thousands of dollars in a tournament where he was seeded first simply because he felt it correct to be honest.

Roddick would not have been criticized if he'd simply accepted the bad call. The ethic in modern, big-time sports is that it's up to the officials to call the game and for the players to abide by those decisions even if they know they succeeded under false pretenses. Andy Roddick went against cultural expectations and instinctively did what he thought was right.

Doing what is good and right and proper, even at personal cost, cost Andy Roddick a lot that day. Yet, he strengthened his personal integrity and won a lot of followers.

As leaders, it can be very easy to fall into the trap of going through our days on auto-pilot – especially if we have been told that we're good leaders. What we fail to realize in this mode of thinking is that we are losing out on opportunities to make even better choices and to have a greater impact.

Many managers make decisions based on intuition and experience. They may gather some feedback, but many times they filter it through their internal belief system. Agile Leaders gather and access data and are inclusive of different perspectives. They seek to understand and engage alternative points of view prior to jumping to a conclusion. They make better choices!

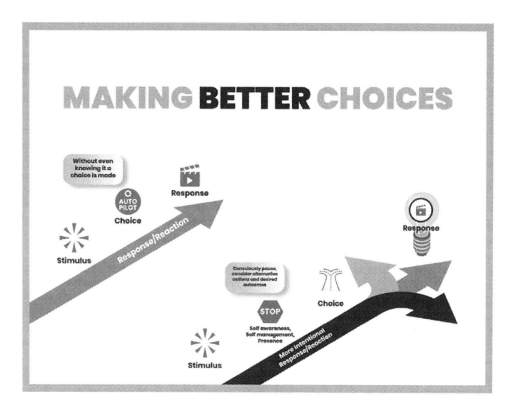

There are millions of stimuli that we are presented with throughout the day. When we are on auto-pilot, we make a choice without even realizing it, and from that choice, we respond or act.

When we're asked, for example, "How was your weekend?" and we respond with "fine," we have faced a stimulus, made a choice on auto-pilot, and then responded. This, however, shortchanges both ourselves and others in developing meaningful relationships.

In order to make better choices and therefore give better responses, we need to slow things down a bit to reflect on what our intentions are and what outcomes we're seeking for ourselves and for others. This pause can be an unrecognizable short span of time, or something a little longer.

The key is to pause long enough to inactivate the auto-pilot and instead reflect on other choices. In this situation, when asked "How was your weekend?" you pause, make eye contact with the person, and respond, "It was great. I had the opportunity to spend some quality time with my parents, which I haven't done for a while. How about yours?"

The choice to share more information and ask the person about their weekend demonstrates a willingness to share and an interest in them as an individual.

Pausing to inactivate auto-pilot, reflect, and consider the choices we have, gives us a greater chance of responding in better ways and achieving the results we seek. Better choices lead to better actions and better results. What kind of choices are you making?

Reflection Questions

- What shadow does your leadership style cast on others?
- How consistent are you at making and meeting your commitments to others?
- Think back to some of the recent choices you have made. What could you have done differently?
- How do you think personal integrity impacts your effectiveness as a leader?

5
LEARNING AGILITY

*The only person who is educated is the one who
has learned how to learn and change.*

—Carl Rogers

There have been many events throughout history that have dramatically altered how people live and work.

Some of the most transformational in the United States over the last 200 years have been the Industrial Revolution, the Transcontinental Railroad, the assembly line, two world wars, the Great Depression, and the Computer/Internet Age.

We're currently living in a very transformational time – with the digitization and democratization of information, and most recently, the COVID-19 pandemic. These two events together have already dramatically altered the way people learn and work.

Given the outcome-uncertain environment we're living in today, Learning Agility has clearly emerged as an attribute that leaders must possess. It may very well be the most important attribute you can develop as a leader today. Organizations are changing so quickly that if their leaders are not agile learners, they're going to fall behind and find it increasingly difficult to catch up to those who are.

David F. Hoff, co-author of *Learning Agility: The Key to Leader Potential*, recognizes Learning Agility as an important differentiator when assessing talent today.

"I'd argue that Learning Agility is one of the most exciting, game-changing concepts in the field of talent management today. Those of us who want to stretch

ourselves at work can examine our strengths and take concrete action to develop our weaker skills. By doing so, we can reach our untapped potential."

Global Workplace Analytics estimates that in 2020, 56 percent of the U.S. workforce holds jobs that are compatible, at least in part, with remote work.[43] Their prediction is that the longer people are required to work at home, the greater the upswing in the adoption of remote work guidelines and practices.

They estimate that 25 to 30 percent of the workforce will be working at home on a multiple-days-a-week basis by the end of 2021. That's a dramatic increase in a very short period of time. As of June of 2020, 3.6 percent of the employee workforce works at home half-time or more.[44] That rate continues to increase as organizations consider safety, cost savings, efficacy, and efficiency.

Not only is Learning Agility essential for leaders to be able to adapt to changes in talent management, but it is vital for leaders and their ability to acclimate to considerable changes underway in world events, workplace structures, and employee interactions.

McKinsey & Company's report, *The Five Trademarks of Agile Organizations*, suggests that organizations have shifted from "hierarchical structural machines" to that of "living organisms," where leaders will need to lead across functions from the middle.[45] McKinsey identifies this structural change through four trends: [46]

1. *A quickly evolving environment* of stakeholders' and investors' demands, which results in acquisitions and restructurings.

2. *The constant introduction of disruptive technology* such as machine learning, the Internet of Things, and robotics.

3. *Accelerating digitization and democratization of information* requiring organizations to rapidly engage in multidirectional communication and collaboration with employees, customers, and suppliers.

4. *The new war for talent,* which is more diverse than ever.

Interestingly, McKinsey's report was released in 2018. We imagine a fifth trend has emerged since then, leading us even further away from hierarchal structures, as remote work becomes more established due to the coronavirus.

Agile Leaders adapt their leadership and management styles knowing that they have to engage with diverse people with diverse ideas in many different levels and areas within an organization. You have to be able to learn and adapt so that you can bring others along and inspire them to trust and follow you.

We're in the midst of a huge generation shift where Baby Boomers and older Generation Xers are ebbing out of leadership and management and Millennials and Generation Zs are flowing in. Leaders who cannot adapt and learn from the diverse workforce that's coming up may have a difficult time attracting and retaining talent, staying ahead of the marketplace, and succeeding.

In order for leaders to act on this, they have to recognize the need for change, be self-aware, have the desire to understand and adapt, and most importantly, apply what they've learned. Organizational psychologist Dr. David Smith notes that Learning Agility requires three actions from the learner: [47]

1. **The Potential to learn.** Learners must be open to learning and receptive to what's taught to them.

2. **The Motivation to learn.** They must be willing to participate in the learning process.

3. **The Adaptability to learn.** Through reflection on the relevance of the acquired skills and competencies, they must be able to take what they've learned, apply it to constantly changing conditions, and even develop new competencies.

A key differentiator of talented people who truly have high potential is their ability to learn and grow from their experiences. They absorb concepts quickly, and at the first opportunity, apply what they've learned. As those skills and competencies become obsolete, they learn new ones to adapt to change. This is why Learning Agility is a critical attribute of Agile Leaders.

An example that comes to mind is of a former colleague, Marcus. Marcus was the Director of Park Services at a nationally-known theme park. Every year, new restaurants, attractions, games, rides, and general renovations were planned for the park.

Marcus was rarely involved in the planning, but because of his Learning Agility, was always prepared to adapt his processes and staffing models to accommodate changing guest interests and the direction of traffic patterns in the park.

Like many middle managers, Marcus had to "deal with" the changes. However, he was an agile learner. He understood who the decision makers were and he spent time understanding the strategy and why particular decisions were made.

Most importantly, he was able to apply what he learned, inject himself into the process, and influence the decisions made. Marcus learned the best approach to shaping change and became a champion of the process.

Identify and assess organization-wide agility and establish Learning Agility as a priority in your approach to identifying talent. In this fashion, you'll be able to build organization agility that aligns with key strategic priorities; you'll win when confronting today's volatile and complex business landscape; and most importantly, you'll drive performance by consistently placing highly Agile Leaders into critical roles.

Characteristics of a Learning Agile Leader

Learning Agility, sometimes described as "knowing what to do when you don't know what to do," requires an open and receptive mindset. Those who demonstrate strong Learning Agility often excel at being able to study, analyze, and understand new situations and new business problems.

Learning Agility involves the ability and willingness to learn from experience and to then apply that learning to perform successfully in new situations. Research from the Center for Creative Leadership has determined that a major difference between successful people and those whose careers falter is their ability to translate meaning from their experiences into changes in behavior.

Korn Ferry research shows just how vital Learning Agility is to successful leaders, potentially more than IQ, EQ, or educational background. It also illustrates how important Learning Agility is to organizations: [48]

- Leaders with high Learning Agility are identified as top potential leaders 18 times more often than those with low Learning Agility.
- Executives with higher levels of Learning Agility, and tolerance for ambiguity, empathy, and social fluidity are five times more likely to be highly engaged.
- Individuals with high Learning Agility are promoted twice as fast as individuals with low Learning Agility.
- Companies with highly agile executives have 25 percent higher profit margins.

The focus of talent professionals and leaders must shift to finding and developing people who consistently demonstrate the ability to replace skills, perspectives, and ideas that are no longer relevant and learn new ones that are.

Agile Leaders welcome the speed and flexibility of learning. They're curious, consciously reflective, and open to feedback. They're tolerant of mistakes and are able to undergo the difficult task of unlearning.

Every organization has what we call *Energizers*. These are people who are your real go-getters. They learned early in their career that with hard work and the right relationships, they could achieve virtually anything. They learned what buttons to push and when to push them. They are usually known as the ones you go to in order to get things done and done right. One of the reasons they're successful is because they seek to understand.

These Energizers show up as competent and confident people and show a willingness and ability to apply learning to perform successfully. These leaders are the most successful at inspiring others in the midst of new and ever-changing conditions.

Most interesting about David Hoff's book cited earlier is that Learning Agility is an attribute present in each of us and can be measured on an individual level.

> *"There is an overall level of Learning Agility that everyone possesses. Learning Agility can be likened to a reservoir of energy, and some of our reservoirs are fuller than others. Fullness equates to an energy or inclination to put yourself in situations that require you to do something you haven't done before."*

To summarize, we have found these behavioral characteristics common among agile learners:

- Strong problem-solving skills
- Fast learner
- Seeks to understand
- Interested in personal development
- Intuitive and patient
- Colors outside the lines
- Tolerance for ambiguity

- Conflict management skills
- Good character judgment
- Independent thinker
- Commitment to the team
- Strong self-awareness
- Empathetic
- Respects and is respected

How you learn begins with establishing the right mindset, for our mindset has a direct bearing on our beliefs and the actions we take.

The Five Dimensions of Learning Agility

Korn Ferry Lominger divides Learning Agility into five dimensions.[49] Not everyone is going to have the same skill set in each dimension; we all have our strengths and weaknesses and can be agile in different capacities.

1. Mental Agility

Individuals who rank highly in Mental Agility aren't just intellectuals. The group includes those with street smarts as well. These are the curious, investigative types who move quickly to collect new information, identify its uses, and then apply it in practice. They know how to weed through the fluff and find the healthy root of a resource, turning it into action items to boost their productivity and work toward their goals.

Mentally agile people take complex situations and break them down into something that they can apply in practice. They are more inquisitive and curious about what the options may be. They don't get bogged down in the complexity of things and are able to articulate things to others so that they can get others engaged and following.

2. People Agility

This dimension refers to one's social skills. Are you comfortable interacting with people? People Agility allows individuals to build strong relationships easily and connect on an emotional level. They're often the first people whom others turn to when problems arise. They're great at navigating difficult situations and adapting to change.

Those with People Agility are able to work with just about anyone. The McKinsey study we cited earlier shows how the generational shifts that are taking place in the workforce are requiring leaders to be able to adapt their style to the workforce coming up. Agile Leaders are constantly developing relationships and are inclusive of others' diversity of thoughts and practices. Such inclusive attitudes and relationships build trust and lead to higher performing teams.

3. Change Agility

Leaders with Change Agility love a good challenge and tackle new experiences head on. They're experimental and like to use different perspectives and methods to solve problems. Often seen as go-getters, there's little that will stand in their way when searching for a solution. With Change Agility, there's no fear of failure – only the excitement to learn something new.

Agile Leaders first understand the change and then determine how they're going to transition through it. They then articulate to others the need to change and help them to transition more successfully. The most important thing is that Change Agility is more about the self than others.

Agile Leaders have an internal voice that either convinces them that they need to take action or not. They're able to manage that self-talk, embrace the change, and transition into something that helps them move forward.

4. Results Agility

Results Agility characteristics are fairly similar to those of Change Agility, though there's one distinct difference. While people who score high on Change Agility have the mindset of getting back on the horse, those with Results Agility aim to never fall off in the first place.

The perfectionist twin of Change Agility, these individuals are just as passionate about new experiences, but have a second drive that pushes them to get the best results possible every time. Instead of trial and error, it's trial and nail it.

There are people who make excuses for the results. Then there are people who say, "All right, here's what it is now. What are we going to do to address it?"

Leaders with Learning Agility take the latter approach, which acknowledges that "It is what it is. I may not like it and I don't want it to be this way, but here's what we're going to do to fix it."

5. Self-Awareness Agility

Self-awareness is the ability to identify and understand your own strengths and weaknesses, and is actually incredibly important to one's career success. Those who are self-aware typically perform better than others because they self-assess and adapt accordingly. Their lack of blind spots makes them invaluable in work settings because they carry an objective view of situations and often offer an unbiased perspective.

Being aware of the *Five Dimensions of Learning Agility* can help leaders to better allocate resources and assign roles accurately by allowing team members to be productive and efficient based on their Learning Agility profile. A common and significant characteristic in all of the *Five Dimensions of Learning Agility* is mindset.

Fixed vs. Growth Mindset

In Chapter 1, we shared how "mindset" as a concept has received a lot more consideration in the last decade as compared to 20 or 30 years ago. Mindset can be described as an attitude or state of mind; an inclination, disposition, or mood; or simply a way of thinking. The reality is that our mindset has a direct bearing on our beliefs and the actions we take.

Fixed vs. Growth Mindset

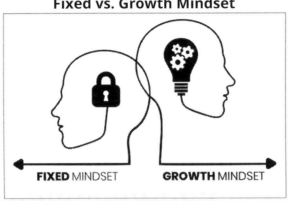

In a Fixed Mindset, people believe their traits are set and therefore cannot be changed. These people document their intelligence and talents, rather than working to develop and improve them. They also believe that talent alone leads to success, and effort is not required.

Alternatively, in a Growth Mindset, people have an underlying belief that their learning and intelligence can grow with time and experience. When people believe they can learn, they realize that their effort has an effect on their success, so they put in extra time, leading to higher personal achievement. To be learning agile, you need to have a Growth Mindset. You need to be open to learning from mistakes and to learning through change.

Through our work and research, we have identified the 10 most productive strategies for linking Growth Mindset and Learning Agility.

Ten Strategies for Linking Growth Mindset and Learning Agility

1. Demonstrate humility and acknowledge and embrace your gaps.
2. View challenges as opportunities.
3. Know your learning style and use the right learning strategies.
4. Cultivate a sense of purpose.
5. Focus on depth of learning versus speed of learning.
6. Improve ability to listen and apply feedback.
7. Failure is a learning element, don't be afraid of it.
8. Leverage reflection after learning experiences.
9. Have the courage to make a change.
10. Never stop learning – be genuinely curious.

This difference in mindset should lead to differences in behavior as well. If someone believes intelligence and ability are absolute, they're not likely to put in much effort to change their attitude and behavior. Conversely, those who believe they can change these traits may be much more willing to put in the extra time and effort to try to achieve more ambitious goals.

With a growth mindset, individuals may achieve more than others because they tend to worry less about seeming smart or talented, and put more of their energy into actual learning.

While the benefits of cultivating a growth mindset are clearly desirable, a renowned expert in mindsets, Dr. Carol Dweck, is quick to point out that it's not just about telling yourself (or others) that you can improve. In her book, *Mindset: The New Psychology of Success*, Dweck points out three common misconceptions she has encountered:[50]

1. *"I already have it, and I always have."* Dweck warns that a Growth Mindset is not simply being open-minded or optimistic or practicing flexible thinking; it's more specific than that.

2. *"A Growth Mindset is just about praising and rewarding effort."* Although praising and rewarding effort is generally a good idea, it also must be undertaken with an eye on outcomes. Effort that is unproductive is not to be rewarded, and learning and progress should also be met with praise.

3. *"Just espouse a Growth Mindset, and good things will happen."* Advocating a Growth Mindset is a positive step that can lead to positive outcomes, but it's not a guarantee. The mindset needs to be backed up with effort applied to worthwhile activities, and even then, success is not inevitable.

Picture this scenario. You discuss your performance with your manager and receive negative feedback. Your manager has discovered a number of mistakes in the work you're doing and feels that you're not committed or making the effort to deliver a successful result.

If you had a fixed mindset, you may decide that your manager doesn't know how to do the job and therefore completely disregard the feedback. You also may demonstrate skeptical behavior and think, "I just can't do anything right. I don't have what it takes to be successful."

If, on the other hand, you had a growth mindset, you would read the situation differently. Your response would include reflecting on the feedback, taking it seriously, evaluating it as objectively as possible, and seeking out additional information and feedback. You would come up with possible solutions to improve performance and make sure changes are put into practice.

Recent advances in neuroscience and brain plasticity have shown that the brain is far more malleable than ever thought possible, and that connectivity between neurons can change with experience. With practice, neurons can grow new connections, strengthen existing ones, and build insulation that speeds the transmission of impulses.

These neuroscientific discoveries have shown that we can increase our neural growth by the actions we take, such as using good strategies, asking questions, and practicing. It turns out, if you believe your brain can grow, you behave differently. Studies prove you can indeed change your mindset from fixed to growth, and when you do, it leads to increased motivation and achievement.[51]

If you demonstrate Learning Agility with a growth mindset – for the two are so often linked, then your next effort is to determine the most effective way to continue to learn. This is where the Learning Acceleration Model becomes a valuable tool.

Learning Acceleration Model

How do you build Learning Agility and become a more Agile Leader? A research-based, time-tested guideline for developing people, the 70-20-10 Approach, continues to help us understand how people learn, grow, and change over the course of their careers.

The underlying assumption is that leadership capability is cultivated in those who intend to lead *On Purpose*. Learning Agility is a balance of a leader's ability and willingness to learn from experience and also to apply that learning into practice.

The 70-20-10 Approach explains three types of experiences to accelerate learning. We refer to it as the Learning Acceleration Model:

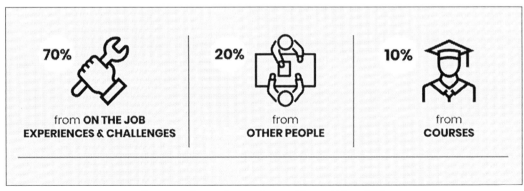

70% from **ON THE JOB EXPERIENCES & CHALLENGES**   **20%** from **OTHER PEOPLE**   **10%** from **COURSES**

Learning Acceleration Model

On-the-Job Experiences & Challenges –
70 Percent

Seventy percent of development occurs by doing. The model's creators believe that hands-on experience – the 70 percent component – is the most beneficial because it enables people to discover and refine their skills, make decisions, address challenges, and interact with influential people such as bosses and mentors. They also learn from their mistakes and receive immediate feedback on their performance.

Listed below are some opportunities that are experiential and relevant. Many of these suggestions are activities you and others can do in your current roles.

- Spend time in a different function or site
- Take on stretch assignments/expanded responsibilities
- Lead new projects or assignments
- Participate in committees/work groups/presentations
- Embrace cross-training/collaborating

Other People – 20 Percent

Twenty percent of development occurs through others in a variety of activities that include social learning, coaching, mentoring, collaborative learning, and other methods of interaction with peers and others. Encouragement and feedback are prime benefits of this valuable learning approach. Opportunities to grow through others include the following activities.

- Seeking out or being a mentor
- Seeking/providing feedback or coaching from/to others
- Discussing and planning application opportunities of key learnings from formal development opportunities
- Participating in professional organizations

Coursework and Training – 10 Percent

Ten percent of development occurs through formal and informal coursework, reading, and training – a concept that typically surprises people. This often is the first place where people turn for development. Yet, there are other ways to learn and develop that are much more effective. Learning activities that fall into this category include:

- Classroom, instructor-led, or self-directed learning
- Open enrollment programs, online learning
- External programs
- Leadership/technical course work
- Books/journals/self-study

The 70-20-10 Approach seems simple enough, but you need to be mindful of the conditions. For example, all experiences are not created equal, so you'll need to determine which experiences will contribute the most to the identified areas of learning and growth. You'll also need to define the leadership lessons to be learned from each experience.

The 70-20-10 Approach continues to be recognized by organizations throughout the world and is considered to be of greatest value as a general guideline for organizations and leaders seeking to maximize the effectiveness of their learning and other development efforts.

Learning is one element though. To be an agile learner, you must make the connections and apply the learning to your daily activities and behaviors.

Why Learning Agility Matters in Management

The one constant in organizations is change, whether the result of technology, emerging markets, societal changes, or diseases. The reasons are as endless as change itself. Leaders with Learning Agility can recognize those changes and get in front of the events and trends. They not only adapt their mindset and behaviors to the change, but help others adapt their mindset and behaviors as well.

You can see this in the number of companies that have stepped up and adapted their assets during the COVID-19 pandemic by shifting their manufacturing lines to produce Personal Protection Equipment (PPE) and ventilators.

In March of 2020, Ford Motor Company was forced to halt automobile production in North America because of the pandemic. It was the first time the automaker closed its plants since World War II. Company leadership called the White House and asked: "How can we help?"

Within two months, Ford's Rawsonville Component Plant in Ypsilanti, Michigan had produced 50,000 ventilators and became the leading manufacturer and exporter of ventilators anywhere in the world.[52]

Rawsonville's leadership determined what their plant excelled at and adapted those skills to keep their employees working by producing life-saving medical equipment to U.S. based hospitals, and ultimately to hospitals around the world.

One question we ask you to consider: why do some leaders have initially successful careers that then plateau or derail? Our experience shows that they tend to "overplay" their experience with legacy solutions. They develop blind spots to their own gaps; they do not work to develop their talents and skills; they often struggle with relationships; and they refuse to relinquish control. They simply quit learning and do not help others continue to learn.

Agile Leaders need to be hungry and restless. Learning Agility is not so much about what someone has accomplished, it's about what they have the potential to accomplish, especially when faced with new challenges.

A key takeaway from Learning Agility is that once leaders become learning agile, their first responsibility is to develop the behaviors that will help them to develop others at different levels, in different situations, and for different reasons. For the ultimate intent of leaders *On Purpose* isn't to attend solely to their own development, but to attend to the advancement of others in the organization.

We'll delve into this further in the next chapter, Coaching Others.

Reflection Questions

- Have you demonstrated a level of self-awareness and humility regarding your development opportunities?
- Have you truly applied what you have learned in recent development experiences? How can you do that more consistently?
- How open and receptive are you to different ways of doing things?
- How would you assess your personal mindset? Growth or Fixed?

6
COACHING OTHERS

Leadership is providing inspiration and vision, then developing and empowering others to achieve this vision.

— *Marshall Goldsmith*

We believe "coaching" is one of the most generalized terms in the business world today.

Although coaching is intended to help people improve their performance, outside of sports, the practice now seems to be applicable to most anything that involves manager-employee relations, making it one of the most misapplied and undervalued variables in the development of people.

Coaching Others is about leaders who empower and support their people in ways beyond using direction or management. We believe it's an attribute that speaks more to having the right development conversation at the right time and allowing others the opportunity to be part of the solution. It therefore makes our top six attributes of an Agile Leader.

Coaching Others focuses on the leader as an advocate of developing others and shares insights into how to create a leadership style that produces positive, growth-oriented outcomes. This attribute, perhaps more so than any of the other five, has as its end game the advancement of others as well as ensuring alignment in the execution of the organization's goals and strategies.

The reasons why leaders might want to cultivate the skills and experiences of others is explained in The McKinsey & Company report we cited in Chapter 5. It describes how organizations have shifted from top-down hierarchies to those of living organisms where authority and decision-making are pushed down, distributed, and localized.[53] This will require individuals to have the competence and confidence to participate in running their organizations.

Agile Leaders prioritize feedback, mentoring, and coaching when engaging with others. They actively develop people to strengthen the organization's talent pipeline and promote each individual's abilities and aspirations. They empower others to act by removing any obstacles to their performance. Agile Leaders allow their people the freedom to make their own decisions and know the feeling and experience the outcome from making the right ones. People are also allowed to make mistakes and know the feeling of accountability, to learn and grow in their capabilities, and to mature into potential future leaders.

As we shared in Chapter 3, John Maxwell recognizes this in his book, *21 Irrefutable Laws of Leadership*. He made people development the first law: The Law of the Lid. [54]

Place crickets in a jar, put a lid on that jar, and they'll jump as high as the lid will allow. Raise or remove the lid, and they'll rise to the occasion and jump even higher. Leaders need to be careful not to be the lids that restrict their people from jumping as high as they can jump or growing as far as they want to grow.

As a leader, how do you expand the capabilities of the people on your team so that they can continue to grow and meet the capacity needed by the organization? Agile Leaders such as Juan and Tasha create a space that enables their people (as well as themselves) to learn and grow and develop their capabilities.

Juan and Tasha

In this chapter, we'll tell the story of two mid-level leaders, Juan and Tasha, and of our work with them in their development as leaders. We'll illustrate opportunities for these two leaders to develop their people through the three key practices of Feedback, Mentoring, and Coaching.

Juan is a great salesperson who several months ago was promoted to a mid-level leader position in his organization and now supervises a group of sales professionals doing the job he used to do. The territory he's responsible for has been underperforming. And he has identified some gaps that his team needs to develop to improve their performance and meet their quota.

Tasha is a mid-level leader whose team is an average-performance team. While they aren't hitting their stretch goals, they're adequately meeting the expected levels of performance. Tasha's frustrated because she believes in her people, but the approach she's been using just hasn't motivated the team to a higher level of performance.

As we continue these stories in Feedback, Mentoring, and Coaching, we'll illustrate the common mistakes leaders often make when developing others. We can all relate to making mistakes, and identifying and defining them creates extremely valuable learning opportunities by having development conversations.

As an example, with all the best of intentions, many leaders will say they're coaching employees when they place them on disciplinary plans and instruct them on the behaviors that they should or shouldn't be engaging in. In our view and practice, as well as in how the practice of coaching is defined, that's not coaching. Disciplinary plans are, however, a very valuable development tool for expectation-setting in which a coaching approach can be utilized.

It's a myth that leaders can only develop others or make them more productive by giving them the answers or showing them how to do the work. Leaders can make the mistake in believing that "being a leader" means having to have the answers and that "helping others" means providing them with solutions. We believe people desire autonomy so they can grow in their own ability to solve problems and make decisions and reap the rewards for success or be accountable for their own mistakes.

The true art of developing others in the business world requires leaders to select the right approach and tool for the specific situation and individual involved. It's not about managing or directing the efforts of others. Rather, it encompasses meeting people where they are in their expertise and skill level, and working with them to expand their knowledge, confidence, problem-solving, and decision-making abilities.

The better leaders become at asking questions and listening, the more consistent people will be at accomplishing mutually satisfying objectives, at feeling empowered, at reducing their resistance to change, and at developing from within themselves a willingness to pursue innovative change.

That is really at the heart of Coaching Others.

Key Concepts in the Development of Others

Imagine a toolbox full of methodologies that a leader can use in developing others. Just as a contractor wouldn't take a ball pein hammer to a job that requires a sledgehammer, you wouldn't take the approach of mentoring when direct feedback is really what's needed. Leaders need to be mindful and intentional about the tools they take to and the conversations they have in each particular situation.

While many leaders view Feedback, Mentoring, and Coaching as essentially the same, we view them as quite different. We are going to share our definition of these three concepts and illustrate when to use each through our leadership development vignettes with Juan and Tasha. We'll then share what we believe are the best practices for these two leaders for giving feedback, mentoring others, and using a coaching approach with their people.

Self-Talk

Self-talk is something we seldom stop to think about. It's that little voice in our heads that causes us to act in ways that align with our thinking. Negative self-talk about ourselves or others can lead to no action or to negative or nonproductive action. Positive self-talk, on the other hand, can increase energy and optimism, and help drive more productive, engaging, and rewarding actions and behaviors.

The two biggest challenges for leaders in developing others are having the will to develop others in the first place and being aware of what their inner voice is telling them.

For example, if a leader is reflecting on an individual, thinking, *"Matt is never going to get it. He makes too many mistakes. I'm not going to waste my time,"* that negative self-talk is going to sway the leader to not take action to help Matt develop. It is in effect a self-fulfilling prophecy.

Through positive self-talk, that same leader could develop an alternative attitude about Matt and his mistakes by thinking instead, *"Matt made this mistake twice before. What do I need to do differently to help him learn how to succeed at accomplishing this task?"*

That alternative inner voice reflects a belief that learning can happen with time and experience and will lead to action that supports Matt's growth and development.

What is your inner voice telling you about yourself?

Is it negative? *"I'll never get that promotion."*

Or is it positive? *"I'm going to learn what I need to do to be more qualified for that promotion."*

What is your inner voice telling you about others?

Is it doubting? *"He is never going to be able to accomplish that task."*

Or is it developing? *"I am going to help him put together a plan to learn how."*

You can view this as a fixed vs. growth mindset as we defined in Chapter 5. Your thoughts can influence the actions that you take, which can impact the beliefs and actions of others. We make this distinction because to be an Agile Leader, one must lead with positive self-talk that springs from a growth mindset.

Feedback, Mentoring, and Coaching are really nothing more than different approaches to a conversation, and checking our self-talk is a way to make sure we approach those conversations with the focus on development. These are all conversations an Agile Leader should be able to have with an individual once they have read the situation and chosen the appropriate approach.

The diagram below depicts the differences between being a consultant, coach, and mentor. We will next share in-depth information about Feedback, Mentoring, and Coaching. Let's begin with Feedback.

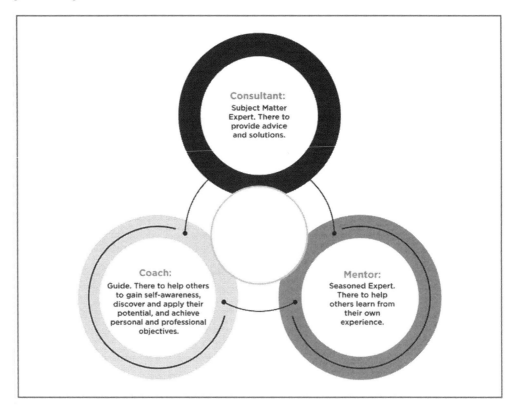

Feedback

Many people don't like to give feedback. They view it as a task and approach it as a task; versus seeing feedback as a gift that can help a person develop. It also helps you develop and succeed as a leader because feedback will create competent, confident people (including yourself) who can do their jobs effectively.

The art of the conversation is in presenting feedback as a gift.

Feedback has to be seen as a developmental conversation, not a disciplinary one. Many people will say, *"I can't give that individual feedback. I don't want to hurt their feelings."*

But if the individual doesn't know they're doing something wrong, how can they improve and grow? Alternatively, if they don't know they're doing something right, how can they know to continue the same behavior?

Some of the mistakes that leaders make in giving feedback include frequently focusing on what someone is doing or has done wrong and not being specific enough when giving feedback. And believe it or not, there are many leaders that feel uncomfortable giving positive feedback. They often believe that it isn't necessary or feel out of their comfort zone complimenting someone. Many believe the compensation someone is receiving for doing the job is recognition enough.

Agile Leaders give positive feedback as a gift that brings attention to the behaviors and actions they want to be repeated, and they give the gift of constructive feedback to help others realize what they've done, the impact it had, and what needs to change going forward.

When to Give Feedback

Carl is a new employee on Juan's team. He has been on the job for three days and is still learning what's expected of him in his new position. For the past two days, Carl has been late for his shift. Juan needs to engage in a feedback conversation with Carl.

Tasha has a person on her team, Lisa, who can do her job with her eyes closed. But for some reason, Lisa made a mistake and a major component failed. Because Lisa has demonstrated her ability to do the job successfully in the past, giving constructive feedback alone would not be the best approach here or effectively uncover the reason for the error.

Simply put, the best time to give feedback is when:

- Someone has done something that deserves acknowledgement and recognition; or
- A certain behavior cannot be ignored due to the impact on others and/or the individual themselves.

Additionally, leaders *On Purpose* know when they themselves should ask for feedback. Two instances that immediately come to mind are when they want to understand how they were perceived by others and when they want to learn more about the impact they had on others. Seeking feedback is a very powerful tool for leaders for their own growth and development.

Mentoring

Mentoring is often used by leaders to develop others by sharing their expertise and experience. Typically, people seek out mentors when they've already gained a bit of experience with something and they're looking for ways to improve their performance.

Unfortunately, as with coaching and feedback, mentoring is often used inappropriately. The idea behind one seeking a mentor is to learn from someone who has expertise in an area one is looking to grow in. Therefore, it's important for leaders to identify the specific area(s) that their people are looking to further develop and then to help find the right mentors at the right time.

People are often encouraged to seek out mentors to accelerate their learning and their development, but little is said about exactly *when* it makes the most sense to have a mentor. Many new to a position are often misguided into believing that they should secure a mentor as soon as possible, even before they start working in their new position. For reasons that will soon become obvious, we believe that is not the best time to mentor someone.

The Right Time for Mentoring

Juan has been learning more about his role as the leader of the sales team. He's finding that he's having a hard time letting go of the "sales" work and embracing his new work as leader. He's tried some things with his team to improve sales performance that have worked for a short time, but Juan is having a hard time making it his normal practice. He's thinking he needs a mentor who's made a similar transition to bounce ideas off of and receive feedback from.

Tasha is having a development conversation with Antonia, an employee on her team. Antonia agrees that she could improve her ability to read and interpret a performance report. However, this is an area that Tasha knows only a bit about and she doesn't feel proficient enough to help Antonia out.

The model presented in the article, *The Perfect Time to Get a Mentor*, and based on the Dreyfus Model of Skills Acquisition, suggests that there is a perfect time for mentorship, depending on where a person is in their level of proficiency.[55]

The model suggests that expertise and skill level can be broken down into five progressive levels: novice, advanced beginner, competent, proficient, and expert. Each of these tiers has a defining characteristic that explains how one operates at that skill level.[56]

1. **Novice** operates primarily on recipes, how-to guides, and other resources.

2. **Advanced Beginner** still uses recipes, but has some contextual understanding of when to use which recipes.

3. **Competent** has an intuition about what will happen and takes personal, emotional responsibility for the outcome.

4. **Proficient** has an intuitive sense of what their goal should be, but not an intuitive sense of what to do about it.

5. **Expert** has an intuitive sense of what they should do and how to do it and largely operates without clear rules.

This points to an important shift that occurs at the **Competent Stage** when a person grows from operating off of rules and guides to operating more off of intuition. It suggests, and we wholly agree, that this is the perfect stage in which to find a mentor. Once someone has done something to a point where they take "personal, emotional responsibility for the outcome," it becomes the perfect time to seek mentoring.[57]

If you try to find a mentor too early, you'll most likely receive more rules and guides to follow. But you could have found those on your own. By reaching out to a mentor after you've already reached the advanced beginner stage, you'll have a repertoire of techniques and tactics that you've learned elsewhere.

Your mentor will then be able to help you hone your intuition about which ones to use when, how to set effective goals, and how to keep improving your intuitive sense of the skill level.

Coaching

There's a reason that leaders are often tempted to give advice and show the solutions. It's usually the quickest way to get things done, and it gets things done in a way that they know will work. As we noted earlier, though, this is not coaching.

Using a coaching approach in the right way in the right situations helps employees develop at work, grow professionally, and become more self-reliant. Coaching increases their accountability and makes them feel valued. Moreover, coaching helps organizations by building employee engagement, reducing turnover, motivating people to work harder, and strengthening the bonds between leaders and their teams.

The practice of coaching involves believing that individuals have, within themselves, the answers to the challenges they face. The coach acts not as a subject matter expert, but rather more of a guide, focused on helping individuals discover and unlock their own potential.

Named the number one thought leader in coaching in 2019, Michael Bungay Stanier calls that temptation the "Advice Trap," the dysfunctional patterns of working that repeat themselves between individuals, within teams, and throughout organizations. He points to the negative repercussions of rushing in to give advice – wasting money, resources, and energy on solving the wrong problems, often with mediocre solutions.[58]

Stanier goes further into the consequences of the advice trap by citing research by business management consultancy Folkman Zender that indicates that leaders who default to giving advice resist feedback from others, are less likeable, and are ineffective at developing others.[59]

Many leaders at all levels are unaware of the amazing power of questions. Many conversations between leaders and their team members may be about requests and demands, but too often leaders are not asking or don't know how to ask the right questions. Moreover, they often don't listen effectively to others' responses to their questions.

As Michael Marquardt notes in *Leading with Questions*, "The better we as leaders become at asking effective questions and listening for the answers to those questions, the more consistently we and the people with whom we work can accomplish mutually satisfying objectives, be empowered, reduce resistance, and create a willingness to pursue innovating change."[60]

When to Use a Coaching Approach

Juan has a salesperson, Parker, who's been quite successful in closing new business, but is struggling recently in asking for the sale. She's seeking out Juan's advice on how she could do things differently. While Juan is tempted to give Parker advice, he knows he needs to help her become more confident in her abilities.

In another situation, Tasha has just participated in a leadership assessment program. While she agrees with what the data is telling her, she has no idea where to begin. She has some thoughts, but can't seem to rein them in long enough to decide what to do first.

According to the *American Management Association*, "When an employee has the skills and ability to complete the task at hand, but for some reason is struggling with the confidence, focus, motivation, drive, or bandwidth to be at their best, coaching can help."[61]

Notice that this definition does not include situations where the employee is lacking the skills or where a behavior continues after several other alternative methods have been used to try to help the employee perform at an acceptable level.

These are the key concepts that underlie Coaching Others, what we believe are the most appropriate times for giving Feedback on performance, for Mentoring others to show them the way, and in Coaching others to finding the solution within themselves.

Let's now continue the stories of Juan and Tasha to illustrate the best practices for each of these approaches that we've refined in our research and practice.

Feedback Best Practices

Having a model to use when giving feedback can be very helpful. It enables you to plan your approach and delivery with the person with whom you're about to give feedback. A template to follow also gives you the best chance of staying focused on your intention for giving feedback and achieving your desired results.

We have found that by using the sequence of the five steps in our **Feedback Best Practices Model**, the planning for and engaging in the conversation with the individual is easier and leads to a more desirable outcome for them as well as for you.

Feedback Best Practices

Start out with an opening statement

Share what you observed

Share the impact the person's behavior had

Ask for their side

Coach on next steps

1. **Start out with an opening statement** as an icebreaker to set a positive, constructive tone. As an example: *"In the past, you've asked me to give you feedback on the presentations that you give. So, I just wanted to talk with you about the presentation you just gave."*

2. **Share what you observed** as a fair, non-judgmental witness. Most importantly, you must be specific as to what you've observed. If you're too general, you won't create a change in behavior because you're not indicating what exactly needs to be done differently. *"When you were giving your presentation, you were looking at the screen more often than the audience."*

3. **Share the impact the person's behavior had** on others, on a customer, on processes, or on the organization as a whole. Many times, people don't recognize the impact of their behavior. *"Because of that, the audience wasn't giving you their full attention."*

4. When you use this model and get to this third step, people's responses are often, "Wow! I had no idea. I'll make sure this doesn't happen again."

5. **Ask for their side** of the story. If you made an observation of someone doing something, that's only one view. The purpose of this step is that before you jump in with recommendations, or before you shift to coaching, their perspective may change the solution. Their perspective may introduce a new element that you hadn't considered. Moreover, you recognizing their reasoning and valuing it is a huge value-add in your relationship with that employee. *"I'm wondering if you noticed the same and what your perspective is."*

6. **Coach on next steps** and the action(s) that they're going to take to ensure the mistake or problem doesn't happen again. It's one thing to flag an issue and show the impact on others, but it's quite another to come up with tangible behaviors that person can implement to create a different, more positive outcome. *"What are some ideas you have on how to avoid that happening in your next presentation?"*

Let's apply these five steps to the different situations we presented earlier in the chapter involving Juan and Tasha. The example dialogue below shows how each of the Five Steps can be applied to Juan's feedback conversation with Carl on being late for work and to Tasha's conversation with Lisa, who, for the first time, had a component fail on her during production. The numbers following the dialog correspond to each of the Five Steps.

Juan's Feedback Conversation

"Hi Carl, I'd like to talk with you about your attendance (1). This is the second time in three days that you've come in late. (2)

"Your coming in late today created a difficult situation with the customer service team who needed to reach you about a very important client situation. (3)

"What is your perspective on this?" (4)

"I'm sorry, Juan. It's hard for me to adjust to my new time schedule."

"I see. While I understand it's difficult to transition to a new schedule, Carl, it's important that you are here when you're supposed to be. What are some things you think you can do to help you get here on time?" (5)

"I'll set my alarm for an earlier time to see if that helps. It's hard getting out of the house because the kids are getting ready for school at the same time. I can also change up my morning routine so I'm not conflicting with the kids getting ready for school."

"I think those are great ideas Carl. Others on the morning shift have found it helpful to get as much ready at night as possible so there isn't as much to worry about in the morning.

I'm glad we had this conversation Carl. I look forward to seeing you here on time going forward." (5)

Tasha's Feedback Conversation

Recall that Tasha has someone on her team, Lisa, who is proficient at her job, but for some reason, Lisa made a mistake recently and a major component failed. Since Lisa had demonstrated her ability to do the job successfully in the past, feedback alone is not going to be effective in helping her learn from the situation.

Tasha begins with feedback and then discovers that a coaching approach could be more applicable and valuable for Lisa. In Tasha's conversation with Lisa, we show how the five steps in our Feedback Best Practices model can be used to identify the problem and solution.

"Lisa, you're very proficient at running your operation, so I know you try to avoid component failures like the one yesterday. (1)

"The component failed to operate at the height of production." (2)

"I also know that you know it caused a significant backup with the rest of the team and set us further behind schedule. (3)

"What are your thoughts about what happened?" (4)

"Tasha, I don't know what happened honestly. I feel bad about it but have been going through everything in my mind and can't figure it out."

Once Lisa explained what happened, Tasha asked a series of questions and listened intently to discover what the best approach would be in working with Lisa, who was obviously very competent and may have needed more than feedback.

"Okay, so let's talk about it a little bit to see if we can figure it out. What have you done in the past to avoid components from failing? What did you do differently this time? How can you make sure this doesn't happen again? What help if any from me do you need?" (5)

In both situations, Juan and Tasha used the ***Feedback Best Practices Model*** to plan their conversations with Carl and Lisa respectively. The model allowed them and their direct reports to stay focused on the intention behind the feedback session and on achieving its desired objective.

Mentoring Best Practices

Recall earlier where Juan was realizing how difficult it was to let go of doing "sales" work and know how to best act in his role as sales leader? His objective for finding a mentor is to learn more about his role and how to make that break from individual contributor to leader.

We can use this situation to share best practices for a mentee seeking and engaging with a mentor. Juan's first step is to identify what exactly it is he wants to discover. Next is to identify the right person to help him with that specific need. If Juan doesn't know who that person might be, perhaps his boss or someone else in the organization could help him identify the right individual. Juan then needs to approach that person with a pre-planned summary of his request and ask if that person would be willing to be his mentor.

Assuming that the person agrees, then Juan would be ready to present specifically what he's looking to learn. He would be prepared for every meeting with his mentor so as to be mindful and considerate of the mentor's time. Juan would then take action on the conversations that he has with his mentor and share progress and results each time they meet.

In another part of the organization, Tasha is having a development conversation with Antonia on her ability to interpret data from a performance report. Tasha thought about it more and realized that her employee was not a novice but an advanced beginner who didn't need more rules and guides, but rather fine tuning to develop her competency.

She recalled that Juan was a subject matter expert with performance reports, so Tasha encourages Antonia to ask Juan if he would be her mentor. Antonia agrees and approaches Juan to be her mentor with the purpose of helping her learn more about deciphering performance reports.

Juan agrees and begins planning his first conversation with Antonia, including learning why improving her proficiency is important to her and how she believes mentoring will help her do her job better. His first mentoring conversation with Antonia will also uncover what she believes her strengths and weaknesses are as it relates to deciphering reports.

Based on this best practice approach, Juan orients himself to understanding what it is Antonia wants to accomplish from the mentoring relationship, not what Juan wants to accomplish, which gets to the role of the mentee in a mentor-mentee relationship.

Antonia's whole objective in reaching out to a mentor is to learn more. She shouldn't simply approach Juan asking, "*I could really use a mentor. Would you be my mentor?*" and not have something specific she wants to develop.

Coaching Best Practices

There's been a great deal of research and thought leadership on best practices in Coaching. In our work, the following considerations and style of conversation define our best practice in Coaching. These strongly suggest that you, as an Agile Leader:

1. **Begin by asking questions** that start with "What…?" and "How…?" and you continue to use questions that show interest and a desire to understand the individual better throughout the conversation.

2. **Genuinely listen** using whole-body listening. Listen with your whole body to what you see, hear, and experience including words, feelings, body language, and emotions.

3. **Be comfortable with silence.** Count to eight. There are many people who think that two seconds is long enough for a silent moment, while for others two seconds feels like ten. Our suggestion is for an eight count to ensure the individual is able to reflect and respond without being rushed.

4. **Respect the person and their situation.** Remember that no matter how similar the person and situation may seem to you and your experience, it's nevertheless very different than you and your situation. This mindset can help you contain your urge to give advice and instead engage in a conversation that will allow the individual to find the solution on their own.

Parker, one of Juan's salespeople, had been quite successful in the past in developing leads and closing prospects, but she's been struggling recently. Parker approached Juan asking for advice about how she could do things differently. Juan was tempted to just give Parker advice, but he held back. He could see she wanted help, but needed to understand first what Parker's issue was. This is a perfect formula for a coaching conversation using the Four Steps in our Coaching Best Practices.

Juan and Parker decide to have a lunch meeting and Juan begins the conversation.

"So, Parker, what's been going on and how can I help you?" (1)

"Juan, I'm going to have a hard time making quota this quarter. I've got to get my close rate up. I know I'm better than this, and I can use a bit of help."

"You've done great with closing in the past, Parker. I'm wondering, what's different now compared to the times when you were more successful?" (2)

"I think it's the material, Juan. This new product line is a bit more technical. I don't know if I've had adequate training in it."

Juan probes deeper and listens for Parker's reasoning. *"So, you don't feel confident in your knowledge of the material?"*

"Exactly. It's not a loss of confidence in my ability as a salesperson, but in my knowledge of the material."

Juan then poses a couple of questions for Parker to think through and respond to.

"Parker, what have you done in the past when you needed to learn something new?" (3)

"Well, first I think reading up on the material has always been helpful. Then watching how someone from engineering services would pitch the product to a prospect."

"So how can you use those techniques in this situation?"

"Maybe scenario playing where I could see the pitch better and watch the prospect react and what their objections might be. And then how well the engineer might respond to each objection."

"How will that help you increase your knowledge of the product?"

"It will help me understand it better and would give me more confidence."

"That's a great idea, Parker. What help do you need from me to make that happen?" (4)

That was a best practice in coaching example because Juan didn't give advice to Parker. Juan could have assumed that her challenge was in asking for the sale because that was how Parker had started the conversation. But Juan discovered that that wasn't the case at all. Parker's need to learn more about the product took the coaching conversation in an entirely different direction.

Recall that Tasha had just gone through a leadership assessment process. And although she agreed with the results, she had no idea where to begin. She had some thoughts about it, but couldn't formulate them into an action plan for herself.

This would be the context of a best practice coaching conversation a trusted colleague could have with Tasha using the Four Steps in our **Best Practice in Coaching**.

"Tasha, you've mentioned that you took a lot away from the leadership assessment that you just went through. What comes to mind for you as far as areas to focus on?" (1)

"Well, I think my ability to build trust in others. I need to be clearer with my communications. And I think I need to be timelier in sharing information. Maybe I need to be more open-minded when people share ideas as well."

"Those are four really powerful things to do Tasha. When you think about your current situation, which of those would you give the highest priority?" (2)

This encourages Tasha and gives her the time to think through highest priority based on her own interpretation of her assessment. (3)

After a brief moment of silence, Tasha identified what she needed to work on the most, based on her own personal knowledge and feeling for her environment, the situation, and the people under her leadership.

"Communicating in a timely manner." (4)

"That's great Tasha. When you think about that priority, when done well, what would that look like?"

We challenge leaders to consider prioritizing feedback, mentoring, and coaching more frequently as distinctive forms of conversation to help build and enable others. Leaders *On Purpose* approach Coaching Others with a growth mindset and willingness to develop competencies and confidence in others.

While Leaders *On Purpose* are aware of their responsibility to develop others and embrace the responsibility at every turn, they're also aware of their responsibility to themselves and their own development. When you fly, flight attendants instruct you to *"secure your own mask first before attending to others."* That may serve as a fitting metaphor for the self-care and self-development leaders should go through as well as helping others in their growth and development.

That really is the best way to ensure there is no "lid" preventing their people from jumping as high as they want to jump or growing as far as they want to grow.

Agile Leaders who can genuinely engage in positive, developmental conversations with their people often possess our next attribute, Followership. Leaders who are able to develop the capabilities and help fulfill the aspirations of their people, gain the commitment of those same people to their purpose and mission. People will trust and show loyalty to leaders who, in turn, show interest in and commitment to their growth and development.

Reflection Questions

- How often do you use open-ended, non-leading questions?
- Are you a patient person? Do you give people the space to think through issues and arrive at a conclusion in the way THEY process information?
- When having a performance discussion, whose agenda are you focused on?
- Do you have a difficult time holding back your opinion in a conversation?
- Have you ever said to yourself or others, "I'm too busy" or "The people I'm saddled with aren't coachable?" How has that impacted your relationship with and development of those people?
- Do you remove roadblocks or simply tell others how to address a problem?

7
FOLLOWERSHIP

Leadership requires followership and following is an act of trust,
faith in the course of the leader, and that faith can be generated
only if leaders act with integrity.

—Lawrence M. Miller

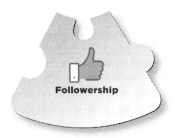

John Lewis was the son of Alabama sharecroppers who, against so many odds, grew to prominence as an American civil rights leader and politician. Though known for being one of the original 13 Freedom Riders and for his Chairmanship of the Student Nonviolent Coordinating Committee (SNCC), Lewis will be memorialized for leading 600 people in Selma, Alabama in 1965 in a march for voting rights across the Edmund Pettus Bridge and into a waiting phalanx of state troopers in riot gear.[62]

Ordered to disperse, Lewis and his followers silently stood their ground. The troopers responded with tear gas and bullwhips and rubber tubing wrapped in barbed wire. The event, named "Bloody Sunday," became a landmark moment in the history of the civil rights movement. Images of Lewis's beating at Selma shocked the entire nation and led to the swift passage of the 1965 Voting Rights Act.[63]

What compelled 600 people to follow John Lewis across the bridge that Sunday morning, all clearly aware of the harm that could come to them?

The moment of truth in this historic event was in their belief in John Lewis. They shared his vision and purpose because he represented them. He galvanized a shared experience and inspired followership in its deepest sense – to put one's self in harm's way.

Some of you may be wondering if Followership is even a word. You know what "Follower" means – someone who gives full support to a particular person, cause, or activity.

Merriam-Webster defines a follower as "One who places themself in the service of another; one who follows the opinions and teachings of another; or one who imitates another."

We like to add a bit more depth to this definition by adding the suffix "ship," indicating a skill or particular character in one's ability to influence others, form relationships, and inspire people to act. It is an ability to connect organizational purpose with each individual and rally the commitment of others to the overall goal. People naturally follow leaders who inspire and are able to articulate a message that aligns with their personal purpose and efforts.

Followership is really the result of demonstrating the other five of the Six Attributes of an Agile Leader: Personal Integrity, Learning Agility and Coaching Others, Systems Thinking, and Change Resilience.

Followership is not about one's title or position in the organization. It is about people believing in you and trusting that you have their best interests in mind. It is also the ability of a leader to have the situational awareness to recognize when someone else is the right individual to take the lead and then to step back or step aside and support them in their leadership of the moment.

Because leaders have such a significant impact on business outcomes, on employee engagement, and on organizational culture, people generally expect them to be dynamic, confident, and visionary. But every leader has to do much more to attain the commitment of followers. Followership has to be earned.

Earning Followership

Pam was not a leader who demanded respect. She was mild-mannered and seemed to always have a smile on her face. Upon first meeting her and engaging with her easy-going nature, people might think to themselves,

> "She can't have that much influence;" I just need to be friends with her and I'll get whatever I want;" or "She's clearly not someone that I need to align with to advance my career."

First impressions could not have been more incorrect. Pam worked at the company for over 20 years and had a deep knowledge of its operations. She knew the office politics, and, although she hated getting involved, knew how and when to push back when necessary. Most importantly, Pam demonstrated a number of behaviors and achieved results that made her a leader who others loved to follow.

Pam demonstrated a genuine respect for others. Although she was a senior vice president and great friends with the CEO, she never relied on her title or influential relationship to get people to follow her. She never used intimidation, negative language, name throwing, or persuasion to get people to do what she wanted. People lined up behind her voluntarily. When you demonstrate a level of respect for others, you gain respect from others.

Pam was the perfect example of courage. Even when faced with tough decisions or challenging times, she was never afraid of being exposed to criticism for her decisions. Confidence and courage are the keys to giving others hope, which is why people choose to follow courageous leaders. If you are fearful and timid of making tough decisions, they will soon know that you are not a sustainable leader.

Pam was rock-steady through good and bad. Agile Leaders understand the importance of being consistent in their nature and standards. There was always a significant level of change, turnover, and transition occurring in Pam's company, and employee loyalty was an important asset for its sustainability. Pam was not a quitter when the going got tough and because of her unassailable nature, had the uncompromised loyalty of others even when it could have a negative impact on them.

Pam was always dedicated to supporting others. People value and respect leaders who add value to them and who show genuine curiosity toward them. They see visible signs that their leader cares about their growth and development.

The result? The people Pam attracted to her team were always the highest performing people in the company. It's not that she hired better than others, it's that people in the organization were drawn to her and aligned around her vision, which aligned with their purpose. They wanted to be there to make sure she was successful, because if she was successful, they would be successful; and they were. Pam's leading *On Purpose* generally led to other's personal success. It encouraged others in the organization to be involved and take calculated risks and do what was required to succeed.

High Performers Don't Follow Low Performing Leaders

People don't follow leaders because they have to. They follow leaders who act with intention and with purpose. A talented engineer is not looking to work for a leader who lacks the proper skills or has a fixed mindset. Rather, people want to follow leaders who continue to grow, support their own growth, and value them for their contributions.

People who love to play a sport such as golf or tennis learn to appreciate playing with someone who's better than they are. This forces them to up their own game and challenges them to work out whatever aspects of the game they need to in order to close the gap.

On the other end of the spectrum, playing against an equal or weaker player is not as challenging. It's probably not as much fun either. There's less to learn from the opponent or learn about the game.

You tend to perform better when those who surround you excel at what they do. Your level of effort and effectiveness is correlated with their level of talent. This is especially true of the impact talented leaders have on others.

People who lead with purpose and an intent beyond their own gain have an innate desire to develop others around them. You might say they are "A" performers who develop "A" talent. John Maxwell's "Law of the Lid" that was introduced in Chapter 3 recognizes the value of leadership and the incredible impact of high-performing leaders on others' effectiveness. The lower an individual's ability to lead, the lower the lid on the potential of others. The higher a person's ability to lead, the higher the lid on others.

If your leadership rates an 8, then your team member's effectiveness can never achieve greater than a 7 rating. If your leadership rating is at a 4, then your team member's effectiveness will never achieve a rating greater than 3. High-performing talent typically don't align with low performing leaders; they want to follow a level-10 leader so they can learn, develop, and grow.

The Measure of a Leader

People have misconceptions about what leadership means. They assume that if an individual has a title such as president, vice president, or director, then they must be a leader. But title alone doesn't make one a leader. The measure of a leader is grounded in their ability to influence others to believe in them and to follow them.

To influence others is to have a direct impact on their opinions, attitudes, and behaviors. But influence shouldn't be confused with manipulating others to get your way. It's about noticing what motivates people and using that knowledge to inspire, build relationships, and build credibility so that people will trust and follow you.

Stephen Covey says that credibility "boils down to two simple questions: Do I trust myself? and am I someone others can trust?"[64] By establishing credibility, you begin to establish trust, which is an essential step in gaining influence with others.

The Great Influencer

President Abraham Lincoln has often been described as compassionate, kindhearted, and immodest, yet became one of the most effective leaders in world history. This is evident in his remarkable accomplishments in taking a stand and changing the hearts and minds of many on the issue of slavery, and then uniting a nation after a brutal civil war.

According to Doris Kearns Goodwin, American biographer and historian, Lincoln's strong influence on friends and foes alike was due to his "extraordinary empathy – the ability to put himself in the place of another, to experience what they were feeling, and to understand their motives and desires."[65]

Lincoln's influence was a cornerstone of his Followership that was sourced from his capacity to recognize the challenges people faced and the sacrifices they made. He profoundly cared about people. He assured people of their individual significance.

Leaders who demonstrate these empathetic behaviors have a good understanding of the world around them, as Lincoln did in hearing the will of a nation. Leaders with Followership know when it's time to lead and when it's time to listen.

To Know When to Follow

Leadership is not about command and control. At one time or another, every leader worth their salt is a follower in some way. Leaders *On Purpose* demonstrate a heightened level of self-awareness and the ability to see those moments, which helps them understand when it is best to step back and let others take the lead.

Followership is about your ability to inspire others to follow, and it's also about you having the humility to admit when you don't know something or there is someone better for the task. It's having the unpretentiousness to step aside and let somebody else take the lead when appropriate. It doesn't mean you're less of a leader; it means you're letting someone with greater talent, skill, or experience lead the team or the project in that moment. That behavior exemplifies an Agile Leader.

Regardless of one's role or hierarchal level in an organization, every individual can have a positive impact on their staff, peers, and even superiors. You can encourage, support, and help each other find the way forward through problems or difficult situations. Setting this kind of example makes you an influential person, regardless of title. The mindset is to aspire to be a contributor, someone who makes possible the success of your company and your coworkers.

Behaviors Anchoring Followership

On Purpose leaders create followers when they practice these key behaviors.

Make Good Choices: Leaders who develop followers have an obligation to the organization and its people to do so in an honest and ethical manner. No one disputes that good judgment is critical to being a good leader. When we see a good track record, we tend to believe it can be done again. Often, this is a correct assumption. Followers respect leaders who have proven themselves in the past and want to be a part of that particular leader's future.

Demonstrate a Strong Work Ethic: Committed followers are strong performers when they see similar behaviors coming from their leader. They are diligent, motivated, committed, pay attention to detail, and make the extra effort. Leaders have a responsibility to create an environment that permits these qualities.

Be a People Developer: It's the obligation of the leader to assure that each individual on their team has the skills to do their job. But this can never be viewed as simply a task or responsibility. It needs to be a passion for people. This will drive Followership.

Lead with Honesty: Transparency and candidly sharing feedback to others garners respect. This is especially the case when there is a level of uncertainty and disagreement. This must contain a balance of respect and directness. Emotions and individual situations must be considered when talking with others.

There is a game commonly leveraged in conflict resolution training called the "Red – Black" Game. The behaviors that traditionally reveal themselves in this game harbor a win-lose mentality. With Leaders *On Purpose*, it's never a zero-sum game where one has to lose in order for another to win. They always seek a win-win result.

Have Courage: Honesty and transparency require a foundation of courage. It takes true resolution to confront a leader about concerns with their agenda or behavior. There's a reason that Churchill called courage, "The foremost of the virtues, for upon it, all others depend." It takes courage to stand up for what one believes is right and to be driven by truth enough to motivate and inspire followers. It also takes courage to respect the courageous moves of others.

Manage Ego: Leaders On Purpose have their egos under control. They are team players in the fullest sense of the term. Success comes from performance and goal achievement, not personal recognition and self-promotion. They understand that personal success comes from the success of others and the organization as a whole. They also are open to and grateful for constructive feedback from others.

We repeatedly witness this in politics. There are many who gravitate toward political careers for the power that comes with the profession and simply don't have the humility, curiosity, or passion needed to be a leader of people. As a result, they often find it difficult to accomplish anything. By comparison, those that demonstrate the behaviors we mentioned above gain followers and are more able to achieve their vision and purpose in their position.

It's the Person, Not the Position

We stated earlier that Followership is not driven by position, title, or level in an organization; it is influenced by the ability of a leader to align and engage people around a purpose and vision. We are willing to bet that you have been witness to people who lead without direct authority.

This was humorously depicted in the 1987 American film, *Secret of My Success*, in which Michael J. Fox portrayed a recent college graduate, Brantley Foster, who, from an entry-level position in the mail room of a large corporation, influenced dramatic change once he realized that the company was about to make some detrimental decisions. Although presented as a spoof, in our work, we've witnessed people without title and authority bring about change in their organizations.

Glenn, as example, was a project coordinator in a large global firm. Although he was an individual contributor at an entry-level position in the company, he was involved in many large projects, in planning meetings, in scheduling resources, and sometimes simply running down to the cafeteria to get lunch for the team. From his position, Glenn was privy to all of the important conversations and listened to each senior leader's perspective. He began asking a lot of questions himself.

Eventually, the senior leadership team started engaging Glenn, as it became clear that he had a depth of understanding of the core issues and offered viable alternative resolutions to issues facing the leadership team. You see, Glenn was able to gather critical information without the filters of his own bias. He truly tried to understand all perspectives. He asked questions and had the courage to challenge the thoughts and positions of others because he had data and information to back up his observations and recommendations.

Glenn was honest and candid. He didn't get offended when others initially disregarded his contribution or opinion. He simply kept asking questions and sharing facts to back up his point-of-view. As projects advanced, Glenn was no longer coordinating meetings and tending to lunch, he was fully engaged in the debate and directly influencing the direction of the project. The magic happened because Glenn, an entry level coordinator, took the time to listen to multiple points-of-view, align with others on the team, and demonstrate a genuine respect for their thoughts and contributions. Glenn became someone the entire team began to follow.

Influence and humility are foundational to the character of a leader who has Followership. People follow the person, not the position. This manner of Leading *On Purpose* is enthusiastic about the work and intentional about forming relationships – behaviors that create followers.

According to John Maxwell in *The 21 Irrefutable Laws of Leadership*, when a group first comes together, leaders tend to focus on what is natural for them to do: lead. Eventually, people change direction to follow the strongest leaders. From there, people naturally align with and follow leaders stronger than themselves. [66]

When followers benefit from being associated with a leader, they'll want to advance alongside that leader. People desire to win and win with a leader they respect.

> *"When people respect you as a person, they admire you. When they respect you as a friend, they love you. When they respect you as a leader, they follow you."*[67]

As we noted earlier, Followership is the result of demonstrating the other five of the Six Attributes of an Agile Leader. We'll see this connection in Systems Thinking, the topic of our next chapter. Leaders with Followership view the organization as a living ecosystem and break down silos and build interactive networks – a mindset that empowers followers to believe they're part of something larger than themselves.

Reflection Questions

- How do people respond when you ask for their commitment?
- Are people ready to follow you and even take risks and do whatever is needed?
- Are they ready to change when you ask for it?
- Do others react to your requests for commitment with doubts or questions, or make excuses?
- How much respect do those closest have for you?

8
SYSTEMS THINKING

Learn how to see. Realize that everything connects to everything else.

—*Leonardo da Vinci*

Charles Handy, an Irish author/philosopher specializing in organizational behavior and management, often spoke about the leadership quality of seeing the bigger picture. To illustrate that mindset, he told a story of a traveler who came across three stonecutters working in a quarry, each cutting a block of stone to be used in the construction of a cathedral.[68]

He asked the first stonecutter what he was doing.

"*I'm cutting a stone!*" he said.

The traveler turned to the second stonecutter and asked him what he was doing.

"*I'm cutting this block of stone to make sure that it's square, and its dimensions are uniform, so that it will fit exactly in its place in a wall.*"

The traveler then turned to the third stonecutter. He seemed to be the happiest of the three and when asked what he was doing he replied,

"*I'm building a cathedral!*"

Agile Leaders, those who lead with the organization and its systems in mind, are not linear thinkers – they are systems thinkers. They understand how things influence one another in the context of the organization as a whole entity, an ecosystem. With this mindset, Agile Leaders know that activities, interventions, or changes in one area have an effect in another area or areas, and even on the organization as a whole.

The following table highlights a number of differences between leaders who think with a linear mindset compared to those who gravitate more toward Systems Thinking.

Leaders as Linear Thinkers	Leaders as System Thinkers
Focus on their respective area or function	Focus on the impact to the organization
Are concerned with tactical issues	Are concerned with process relationships
Try to fix symptoms	Zero in on core causes
Think about impact on self	Think about the impact on others
Are concerned with assigning blame	Try to identify patterns and answers
Control and order to limit chaos	Try to find patterns amid chaos
Care about the content of communication	Care about patterns of communication, content, and interactions
Dislike ambiguity	Accept ambiguity

Organizations are made up of many complex relationships and interrelationships, and today's leaders need to think in terms of the whole rather than focusing solely on their own departments or functions.

As an example, replacing a lower cost component for an engine may have a positive impact on the cost management goals of the sourcing department, but it may negatively impact the quality output and productivity on the production line in manufacturing, the design from an engineering perspective, and the efficacy of the product for the customer.

Systems thinking is the process of understanding how elements influence one another within a structure, which, in essence, describes an ecosystem. Natural sciences such as ecology and geography define an ecosystem as a geographic area where organisms, weather, and landscape, work together to form a "bubble of life."[69]

Organizations are a lot like bubbles of life with divisions, departments, work groups, and individual contributors working together to achieve a shared goal.

As an attribute of Agile Leaders, Systems Thinking sources from a holistic mindset as an underlying view of life. Leaders who are systems thinkers have a sensitivity to the circular nature of the ecosystem of the organizations they lead. They recognize that for every action, there is a reaction, and there are consequences for their actions as leaders and decision makers on others and on the organization.

Systems Approach to Management

Applying Systems Thinking to how you lead guides your ability to analyze each business decision according to the overall benefits and consequences it could have on individuals and parts of the organization.

Leaders who act *On Purpose* are Systems Thinkers when making business decisions because they understand that their resolutions can impact the entire organization and the people who work within it – the entire ecosystem.

Systems Thinking also guides the decisions of *On Purpose* leaders whose aim is to impact the greater organization with their leadership, problem solving, and decision making. They may lead a team or function in a decentralized location but know that they are a part of and responsible for the entire organization's productivity and profitability.

If, for example, the intent of a department head is to buy a new piece of manufacturing equipment, Systems Thinking would lead to analyzing elements such as the effect of downtime for installation of the equipment and employee training on production, revenue, and profit goals for their department and for the company as a whole.

Ultimately, the goal of Systems Thinking is to help leaders avoid wasted time, money, and resources as a result of the decisions they make. A systems approach requires a broader and deeper vision, almost three-dimensional, to view the organization as a set of interrelated and dynamic parts and subsystems in continuous interaction. Similar to an ecosystem, this approach is always optimizing working together to enable the organization to function properly and thrive as a "bubble of life."

Interconnected Parts

Systems Thinking requires a shift in mindset away from linear toward circular thinking. Part of this mindset shift includes understanding and behaving with the belief that everything is interconnected – not in a soft and spiritual way, but in a practical and process-oriented way. The reality is that everything relies on everything else for the survival and success of the ecosystem, even in the simplest of environments.

From a systems perspective, we know that larger things emerge from smaller parts and a successful organization is a result of the sum of its parts. Leaders *On Purpose* make decisions based on the impact of all parts, not simply their area of responsibility.

All organizations are dynamic and often complex. They are no longer hierarchical machines, but living, breathing organisms that thrive on interconnections. Agile Leaders take a more global or holistic approach to leading because they are operating as system thinkers. They try to understand the impact of their decisions on others, even if it makes it harder for them and their team.

This means appreciating the whole and the parts at the same time, along with the relationships and the connections that make up the dynamics of the organization. Essentially, this is the ability to see interconnectedness and the cause and effect of elements on each other and on the organization as a whole. Recognizing causality in systems thinking is being able to decipher, with an overarching perspective, how actions influence other actions and impact results, which in turn shape future actions.

Recognizing Causality in Systems Thinking

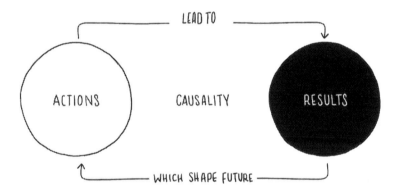

Stu is the Vice President of Operations at a beverage company. In his process for planning the production schedule each calendar year, he spends time with other functions in the organization in order to understand their needs and the impact of his decisions on their ability to service customers.

He could easily decide that he is going to re-engineer his production lines and re-skill his workforce to reduce cost and build efficiency; however, he knows that the decisions he makes will impact the decisions of others in the organization. Stu is a Systems Thinker who makes decisions for the greater good of the organization, not simply for his area of responsibility.

The Impact of Systems Thinking on People

The Martyr Complex is a destructive pattern of behavior where individuals "playing the martyr" have an exaggerated sense of obligation to suffer or sacrifice for others in order to elicit sympathy, love, and admiration. It's also meant to evoke guilt, which is more of a passive-aggressive behavior. These behaviors in a leader often create fractured relationships and poor team performance.[70]

You can see examples of this behavior when *Off* Purpose leaders mislead their people by having them believe that the organization or other leaders are out to get them or set them up to fail. This can also be heard in language used by *Off* Purpose leaders such as "us" and "them." When one of these leaders talks about their team as "us" and the rest of the organization as "them," they are creating a narrowly-focused, divisive environment that is in direct conflict with Systems Thinking.

Once they fabricate this falsehood, they act as martyrs for their teams, sacrificing themselves for the good of their people as a shield against the falsehood they themselves created.

Though not always, a martyr complex in leaders can be a sign of narcissism. They may appear insecure and self-effacing, but are often self-absorbed, vain, and have a feeling of entitlement because of their position or their relationship with senior leadership.[71] They tend to focus on themselves first and have little regard for the impact their decisions have on others. Their ultimate goal is to make certain that they look good or they shine above the rest.

These types of leaders do everything they can to make certain their department performs at optimum levels, taking credit when things go well, yet blaming others when things go wrong. In interviewing these leaders, we often discover that they don't consider or care about what happens to others or the organization as long as they look good.

Conversely, Leaders *On Purpose* tend to see the organizations they work in as an inter-related whole of mutually beneficial subsystems. They act with the best interests of the company in mind. We've seen this mindset in action.

Dan is one of four Regional Vice Presidents of Sales at a pharmaceutical company. His team has outperformed their revenue and profit margin goals in each of the last three years. Dan has eight sales directors reporting to him and three have exceeded their goals by nearly 10 percent in each of the last three years.

Two other regions in the company have struggled, and the organization has determined that they need to replace their regional vice presidents. Dan, knowing that two of the directors on his team are ready to advance as a result of their performance, recommends them for these two critical vice president positions instead of keeping these two high-performing directors on his team.

Dan knows that this could have a potentially negative impact on his region's sales and profit targets, but he also knows the best outcome for the success of the organization is to promote his two people. It's also the best outcome for the growth and development of his two directors and everyone else on Dan's team. Dan is an Agile Leader and Systems Thinker with the greater good in mind.

As an observer, you may be thinking that this was the right thing for Dan to do. Yet time and again, we've witnessed leaders hide their top talent for fear of losing them to another part of the organization. Leaders who are self-centered and harbor a fixed mindset limit the ability of their people to develop and grow. The impact on the organization is lower performance, lower engagement, and lower retention, as skilled and experienced people will want to get out from under leaders to find their own next career step, even if that is outside of the organization.

Leaders who are Systems Thinkers are always thinking ahead, developing their next level of talent, and supporting the overall organization, even if it may hurt them in the short term.

Feedback Loops

In that everything is interconnected, there are constant feedback loops and flows among the elements of a system. We can observe, understand, and intervene in these circles once we understand their type and dynamics.

Understanding feedback loops starts with understanding cause and effect. As we shared earlier, causality as a concept in Systems Thinking is about being able to interpret the way elements influence each other in a system. Understanding causality leads to a deeper perspective on agency, feedback loops, connections, and relationships.

Systems Thinkers understand the interconnectedness of parts. They seek to build relationships with other leaders throughout the organization and collaborate to make decisions. These feedback loops are critical to building an organization that can sustain success over time. These leaders understand that they represent the larger organization and are intentional with their actions. They act *On Purpose*.

Why Use Systems Thinking?

Systems Thinking expands the range of choices available for solving a problem by broadening our thinking and helping us to comprehend and articulate problems to others in new and different ways. At the same time, the principles of Systems Thinking make us aware that there are no perfect solutions and that the choices we make will have an impact on other parts of the system. By anticipating the impact of each trade-off, we can make informed choices and minimize the severity of each, or even use it to a greater advantage.

It is also valuable for telling compelling stories that describe how a system works. For example, the practice of drawing causal loop diagrams forces a team to comprehend shared pictures or stories. Such tools are effective vehicles for identifying, describing, and communicating one's understanding of systems, particularly in groups.

While we have just shared with you the meaning and value of Systems Thinking to an organization, there are nevertheless traditional, often reflexive barriers to becoming a Systems Thinker.

Barriers to Systems Thinking

In our research and practice, we've identified many barriers to Systems Thinking – patterns of learned and, at times, instinctively defensive behaviors that can hinder leaders from seeing the bigger picture. These are the most prevalent and present in most every organization.

1. *The Quick Fix.* This is when a leader jumps on the first solution that pops up, not taking the time or effort to look into root causes. It's essentially putting a bandage on a symptom. Leaders may think they're acting decisively, but often either neglect to solve the problem or end up exacerbating it, costing the organization more time and resources.

2. *Reactive Thinking*. Similar to the Quick Fix, but not always quick, reactive thinkers let their circumstances and conditions control them. Reactive leaders respond to their environment but seldom act on their own. When they do respond to a situation, they often do so without considering other people's points of view or the impact that a decision may have on them and on the organization.

3. *Bottom Line Reasoning*. The primary objective with this line of reasoning is to save money, which can often lead to short-sided decisions that end up costing more in the long run. Budgets are the rational of linear thinkers. They force

themselves and others to make decisions based on money rather than on short- and long-term tradeoffs.

Sometimes, cost considerations are warranted, but leaders can often use "the bottom line" as an excuse not to make a decision and to maintain the status quo. A Systems Thinker may actually see a greater cost savings by interconnecting other departments and work groups for greater cost efficiencies.

4. *Silo-Centered*. This thinking epitomizes not caring about connections to other areas in the organization or the impact on the growth and development of others, and not showing interest in doing anything other than what will help their own area accomplish what they need to.

   Defensive and protective, this line of reasoning is not only non-conducive to Systems Thinking, but in the long run, is detrimental to the sustainability and growth of the organization. It also feeds into the "us vs. them" mindset that can reinforce the martyr complex.

5. *Over-Thinking*. Some would argue that leaders don't give enough thought to issues. Often due to the demands of an always on, fast-paced 24/7 world, most of the complex problems facing society and organizations today are boiled down to a few sound bites on the evening news. A leader that overthinks takes far too much time to make a decision or may be suffering from analysis paralysis. They may tend to be risk-averse and therefore cause delays.

6. *Don't Rock the Boat*. There are people in organizations who always seem to be trying to find accord. They'll do anything to keep the peace, often to the detriment of not solving the issue and allowing it to worsen. Edwin Friedman, ordained rabbi, family therapist, and leadership consultant, calls this "peace-mongering." It refers to the war-like destruction that spineless and people-pleasing leaders create in their communities through their "failure of nerve." Peace-mongers will avoid, suppress, and mask conflict, at the expense of discussing and addressing real issues.[72]

Systems Thinking is easy for some and difficult for others. Some people intuitively think in systems terms and have done so their entire lives. Others have spent their lives thinking in linear, reductionistic, and mechanistic terms.

At first when people start thinking in systems, they can find things to be a bit chaotic. They become overwhelmed by the number of variables and tend to ask, *"How can I do anything if I don't know what effect my intervention will have?"*

This approach usually gives way to a sense of deeper organizational insight as an individual begins to flex their skills in System Thinking.

Advantages of Systems Thinking

There are a number of advantages for leaders who develop a Systems Thinking mindset. The most significant impact is that you can create a workplace that is more efficient because it takes a holistic view when developing or executing strategic initiatives. There are a number of additional mindset shifts that can happen when systems thinking is a core attribute of leadership behavior.

Optimize the Capabilities of People. Understand how your employees interact with others and other functions in the organization. Make sure to make links to the entire system in order to set your team and the company up for success and to make change sustainable.

By using a systems perspective, you can remove unnecessary steps and find effective short cuts which can save your company resources. Take the time to help the people on your team understand the impact of your function on others within the company.

Take a Holistic Perspective. When you work in a specific department, function, or region, you tend to see solutions to problems through the lens of your area or environment. For example, an operations manager considers their capacity to address a problem, an accountant reaches for their calculator, and a quality engineer aligns standards. The key is getting all to think about their role with the greater good in mind.

As a leader, you don't want to have such a narrow, department-specific focus on resolving issues. Instead, you need to take a step back and look at the entire ecosystem and gain a transdisciplinary understanding of the system. This holistic view helps you unlock your creativity and find new ways to achieve your organizational goals.

Discover Interconnectivity. There are workplaces where people from different departments constantly bump into each other. The designers made these buildings to increase interdepartmental communications and cause the kind of serendipity which leads to unusual solutions. With a systems approach, you realize everything is dynamically interrelated. Each person needs their co-workers to achieve success. The systems style of thinking gives you the tools to integrate interconnectivity, creativity, and productivity into your workplace.

Create a Problem-Solving Mindset. Leaders often find themselves actively working to avoid interpersonal conflict or problems that drive conflict. While you should work to minimize negative complications or issues with others, some problems are worth pursuing in extra detail.

Approach Every Situation with a Win-Win Viewpoint. Humans generally have been raised with the idea that you have to win to be successful. Because of this, we sometimes think that winning includes others losing. In life and in business, that is simply not the case. When you play the game of win-lose, eventually, everyone loses.

Leaders *On Purpose*, who look to the success of the system, take a win-win viewpoint. This means accommodating others' needs to determine the best approach for everyone to win. This is hard, as it means sometimes "giving in" to what you want for the benefit of the greater organization.

Solving a complex, system problem could give you a better way of conducting business, result in a new invention, surface a new process, or reduce duplication of effort.

Instead of avoiding complexity, a systems approach helps you see problems as exciting opportunities. These problems offer potential ways to innovate and develop your creativity. Rather than shy away from difficult issues, your employees turn into active problem solvers.

How to Develop Your Ability as a Systems Thinker?

Many people have thought systemically all of their lives. But for the vast majority of us, the jump to Systems Thinking requires time, practice, curiosity, and intentionality. Ollhoff and Walcheski call it "Making the Shift" and suggest a process for thinking in a systems way.[73]

Instead of...	Try...
Instead of blaming someone, ask...	"What are the influences on that person?"
Instead of saying, "I know the answer...	"I have another perspective on the issue."
Instead of focusing on one item...	Look at all the variables that affect that item.

Instead of…	Try…
Instead of looking at the content of what people say…	Look for the process of what they say. How are they saying it? What are they not saying? What are the common themes in the content?
Instead of focusing on negative behaviors…	Look at what is motivating those behaviors or if they are masking a deeper problem.
Instead of just looking at what individuals are doing…	Also look at the dynamics of the system – what forces are pushing individuals toward one thing or another?

Making decisions for the greater good of the company is the responsibility of anyone in a leadership role, regardless of the level. It takes time and practice to develop a Systems Thinking mindset. Developing some of the following habits will help you on your journey to becoming more of a systems thinker and being more agile.

- Seek to understand the big picture.
- Observe how elements within a system change over time, generating patterns and trends.
- Recognize that a system's structure generates behavior.
- Identify the integrated nature of complex cause-and-effect relationships.
- Make meaningful connections within and between systems.
- Change perspectives to increase understanding.
- Surface and test assumptions. Disagreement is good; disagreeable is not productive.
- Consider the issue fully and resist coming to a quick conclusion.
- Consider short-term, long-term, and unintended consequences of actions.

Where Should You Start?

When you begin to address an issue, avoid assigning blame (which is a common place for teams to start a discussion). Instead, focus on items that people seem to be glossing over and try to arouse the group's curiosity about the problem under discussion. To focus the conversation, ask, "*What is it about this problem that we don't understand?*"

Finally, we often assume that everyone has the same picture of the past or knows the same information. It's therefore important to gather different perspectives in order to make sure that various viewpoints are represented and that solutions are accepted by the people who need to implement them. When investigating something, involve people from various departments or functional areas. You may be surprised to learn how their mental models are different from yours and how potentially beneficial they are.

Systems Thinking also heightens your Change Resiliency – the next and final attribute we'll be discussing – by giving you a much broader lens and holistic perspective for leading yourself and others through the inevitable changes faced by an organization and the transitions that employees go through in accepting the change.

Reflection Questions

- Do you look for connections to the decisions you make and the impact they have on others?
- Do you find yourself being open to diverse possibilities or set in your ways based on your experiences?
- Do you see your role as accountable for your function or as a leader for the entire organization?
- Are you able to focus on the purpose for which a system was created, versus the processes and procedures of the system?
- Is short-term success or a long-term sustainable outcome your priority?
- Can you see what is actually happening or only what you want to see happen?

9
CHANGE RESILIENCY

The oak fought the wind and was broken,
the willow bent when it must and survived.

—Robert Jordan

"Change is the only constant in life."

Ancient Greek philosophers – such as Heraclitus, who first penned that observation around 500 BCE – taught valuable lessons that are still amazingly relevant today. When a simple saying has remained alive for over 2,500 years, it is a good idea to acknowledge and embrace its truth.

Change is as much a part of life as breathing itself, and leaders and organizations have had plenty of experience and awareness on the subject. Why then aren't they better prepared to lead change and help others through the transition process? Change as a constant can be a challenging reality for both leaders and followers to cope with and work through.

Change can be large or small and self-initiated or imposed on people. Regardless of what its cause or how significant its extent, there's a lot for leaders to consider when they are faced with change. For this reason, the last, and most often needed, of our **Six Attributes of an Agile Leader** is Change Resiliency.

We intentionally use the term change resiliency versus change management. It means being a leader capable of leading one's self and others through the inevitable changes and challenges confronting an organization, not simply managing a change process.

It could be said that resiliency is the product of a broad perspective that enhances one's ability to recover quicky from change, hardship, or misfortune. It's the capacity to cope emotionally with a crisis or to return quickly to a pre-crisis status. Resiliency is often associated with elasticity, buoyancy, agility, and adaptation.

Resilient people are able to adapt and bounce back when things don't go as planned. They demonstrate flexibility, durability, an attitude of optimism, and, most importantly, an openness to learning. They don't dwell on failures, but rather acknowledge the situation, learn from their mistakes, and then move forward. They take what's happening around them, understand and absorb it, then adapt and apply themselves.

Leading level-headedly through change can seem impossible at times, but the problems associated with change are generally not because of the change itself, but the transitions that are required of one's self and that of others in dealing with the change.

Agile Leaders can more effectively lead others through the transitions associated with change by first building up their own resilience for transitioning through the change. Only then can they begin to build resiliency in others.

Building Resilience as a Leader

Navigating and surviving this complex, often ambiguous, and fast-paced world can be trying on any individual, let alone someone tasked with leading others through these or any other times of change and uncertainty.

The only path for Leaders *On Purpose* is to develop a change-resilient mindset that will sustain their energy level under pressure and give them a level-headedness with which to cope with disruptive changes, bounce back from setbacks, adapt, and aim to excel again.

"Are You Ready, Willing, and Able?"

Korn Ferry executive J. Evelyn Orr defines Change Agility as, "the extent to which individuals like change, continuously explores new options and solutions, and is interested in leading organizational change efforts."[74]

Through our research, we have found that Change Agility must come from your core as a leader. You must have a willingness to change, an ability to change, and the capacity to adapt to change quickly. It's about leaders being real with themselves about how engaged they are in their responsibility for leading others. At the end of the day, if leaders aren't taking care of their own mindset and well-being, they're not as valuable as they could be to other people. If you, as a leader, do not have the right mindset about facing change or disruption, you're not going to be able to bring others along with you.

Paul is a leader at a medium-sized company who was recently tasked with guiding his organization through some very significant changes. In his coaching conversation with Mike, Paul said something that really caused Mike to pause and say, *"Paul, it sounds to me as if you're not completely on board with this change."*

Paul's response was surprising, *"You know, you're right. I'm not."*

If a leader like Paul, in his highly-visible position, is resisting the change in even the slightest way, imagine how that may be impacting the messaging that he's conveying to others in the organization. Even his body language and tone of voice will give him away if he doesn't believe in the change and the benefits the change will bring to others and to his company's success.

That acceptance of responsibility on the part of the leader reminds us of what flight attendants ask of passengers who elect to sit in the exit row: *"Are you ready, willing, and able to assist in the event of an emergency?"*

You might be thinking that many people will sit in the exit row for the leg room only and never expect to have to lead others out of a dangerous situation. We think so too. Just as there are *Off* Purpose Leaders who are only in it for the leg room, there are many *On Purpose* Leaders who accept the role and will step up out of a sense of responsibility for the welfare of others.

Circle of Control and Influence

As you seek to build resilience in yourself as a leader, you need to be aware of where you are in the change transition process and what is and isn't within your control and influence. Often, leaders try to manage things that are outside of their influence and control. They can sometimes duel too long in this area and miss the opportunity to have an impact.

As diagrammed on the following page, if your focus is on those things that are outside of your control and influence, the circle furthest away from your control, your energy, is likely to be negative and wasted.

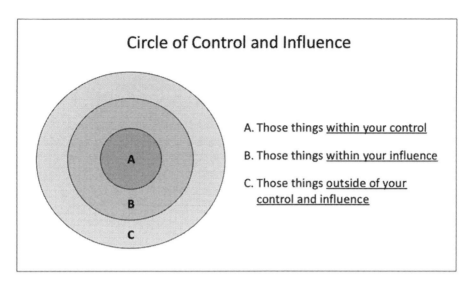

To position yourself in a way that gives you more control and more positive energy, it's important to focus first on the areas that you can control and then the areas that you can influence. The feeling of loss of control is significant during change and times of transition. In working with others, it is also key that you help *them* see what is in fact within their control and influence so they are able to focus on the right things at the right time as well.

Barriers and Openings to Change Resilience

Regardless of how agile you are as a leader, you will naturally have different thresholds compared to other leaders. In our research and practice, we have identified barriers leaders are confronted with in the face of change. We also present the corresponding change-resilient mindset.

Barriers to Change Resilience	Openings to Change Resilience
Lack of clear understanding	Is comfortable with ambiguity.
Competing priorities	Guided by an overarching commitment to their intentions.
Lack of self-confidence	Focused on self-belief as guided by intentions and not fearing failure.
Ineffective or lack of communication	Proactively seeks out and shares information to build strength in self and others.

Barriers to Change Resilience	Openings to Change Resilience
Fear of the unknown	Uses a framework for thinking that challenges conventional wisdom and shows pathways.
Past experiences	Embraces change as continuous improvement and is unafraid of the future. Agile learner who absorbs past experiences to be more prepared.

In our practice, we propose several methods leaders can use to shift their mindset from seeing only barriers to change resiliency to finding openings and a more change-resilient mindset.

Engage in Positive Self-Talk. It may seem trite, but there is science behind positive thinking. Instead of thinking, *"What was leadership thinking?"* ponder instead, *"There's a good reason why the organization is doing this."* Instead of convincing yourself, *"This really stinks!"* reason instead, *"This can help things be better."*

Adapt and bounce forward. Find new ways to continue to move forward. Think outside of the box.

Have a Growth Mindset. Look for opportunities to succeed, not fail. Take the initiative to be/get involved. Have confidence in yourself and others.

Reflect back on situations to identify what worked and what could have gone better. Make note of what didn't work as intended to know what needs to be done differently next time. Pause to enable yourself to make better choices.

In, *Building Resiliency, How to Thrive in Times of Change*, Mary Lynn Pully and Michael Wakefield from the Center of Creative Leadership, state, *"Developing resiliency requires that you pay attention to the complexities of your experiences, listen to your emotions, and be willing to learn from disappointment as well as success."*[75]

Agile Leaders' ability to develop that resilient mindset comes from their Learning Agility, their ability to understand, internalize, and adapt quickly. Resilient leaders have to be agile learners to be able to read and interpret the events around them and then adapt their actions in order to build their resilience.

An Increasingly Uncertain World

Over the past few decades, numerous terms have emerged from business journals and academic literature referring to an increasing inability for leaders to grasp the world and deal with the unprecedented changes occurring around them.

Two recent factors driving extraordinary change are globalization and advancements in technology. Those elements, combined with the speed of innovation and increased competition, make for a world filled with exponential change, requiring more than linear thinking and reasoning.

One of the more well-known terms that has emerged in response to dramatic change is "VUCA," an acronym first used in 1987 and derived from the leadership theories of Warren Bennis and Burt Nanus. It stands for Volatility, Uncertainty, Complexity, and Ambiguity— four different types of challenges that demand four different types of responses.[76]

This framework for thinking was selected by the U.S. Army War College in response to the collapse of the USSR in the early 1990s. Suddenly, there was no longer an "only enemy," resulting in new ways for leaders to view and react to the broader environment around them. Here's a brief summary of the four components of VUCA: [77]

Volatility: The nature and dynamics of change and the nature and speed of change forces and change catalysts.

Uncertainty: A sense of not knowing, the lack of predictability, the prospects for surprise, and the sense of awareness and understanding of issues and events.

Complexity: A state where there are many different elements and connections. The multiplexity of forces and confounding of issues result in no obvious cause-and-effect chain.

Ambiguity: A situation where there is more than one meaning, a haziness of reality, the potential for misreads, and the mixed meanings of conditions; cause-and-effect confusion.

To help make sense of the nature of cause and effect in a dramatically changing environment and how to make decisions within a VUCA environment, the Cynefin Framework is often used. Cynefin, pronounced ku-*nev*-in, is the Welsh word for habitat and "the events in our experience that influence us in ways we can never fully understand."[78]

The framework was created by European IBM Director David Snowden in 1999, along with his colleague Mary E. Boon, to provide decision-makers a context and perspective from which to not only make better decisions, but also to avoid the problems that arise when their default management style causes them to make mistakes. [79]

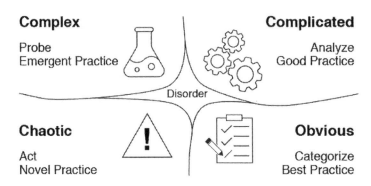

The framework categorizes the issues facing leaders into four contexts as defined by the nature of the relationship between cause and effect. These contexts – Obvious, Complicated, Complex, and Chaotic – guide leaders in how to evaluate situations and act in ways appropriate to each context.

In an Obvious context, there are tight constraints, options are clear, and the cause-effect relationships are apparent to everyone. In other words, the right answer and the best practice is self-evident.

In a "Complicated" context, problems might have several right solutions. There's a clear relationship between cause and effect, but it may not be visible to everyone. The decision-making approach here is to assess the situation, analyze what is known – often with the help of experts – and decide on the best response using good practice.

In a "Complex" context, there is less predictability. Cause and effect are not necessarily linear and often can only be assessed after the fact. The approach here is to step back to see the situation holistically, probe for causes and patterns, sense for developing solutions, and respond with an emerging practice.

In a "Chaotic" context, the relationship between cause and effect is impossible to determine because no identifiable patterns exist. Searching for the "right" answer in this chaotic environment is ineffective. A leader's immediate responsibility is to act to establish order, then respond by working to transform the situation from chaos to complexity, where the identification of emerging patterns and practices can organically reveal themselves.

Agile Leaders wanting to build change resiliency in themselves and in others apply these frameworks for thinking to adapt and adjust themselves and their people in order to outpace their competition or any uncertainty that falls upon their ecosystem.

The COVID-19 pandemic, as an example, threw many leaders and their organizations into chaotic, uncharted waters. Millions of businesses were ended by the shutdowns, but those that were able to stay open and survive had leaders who were change resilient and capable of building that resiliency in their employees. These organizations recovered from the economic uncertainty faster than others.

Building Resilience in Others

One of the first miscalculations leaders make when trying to build resiliency in others is misreading their ability to keep pace. The following graphic illustrates this lag in awareness on the part of leaders of others. Often, a leader will start to experience a change event and can already be onto the next change before the frontline staff even gets a chance to start sorting through the first one.

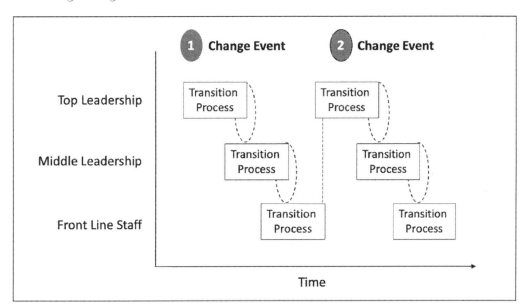

Change is the external event that happens to people. *Transition* is the psychological process that each person goes through in order to deal with and accept the change. The "change plan" for an organization may address important things, such as process, communication, and technology. However, the "plan" seldom addresses the transition journey that each individual impacted by the change goes through.

Take, for example, the implementation of a new software system, or perhaps bringing in a new boss, or even, for the foreseeable future, changing from working at the office to working from home. The change starts with the preparation for the "new" and ends once it's been implemented; i.e., the software systems go live, the new boss is in place, and people have created a workspace at home.

What few organizations consider is outside of the training on the new system, the introduction to the new boss, or the setup of a home office, there are many other elements to consider for people to transition successfully. Many leaders think that once the change is made, they don't need to focus on it anymore, when, in reality it is just the beginning of the change-transition process.

In the area of acknowledging and planning for change and transition, William Bridges' work stands out as very powerful. The "Bridges Transition Model" has been used by leaders and management consultants for more than thirty years. It helps organizations and individuals understand and more effectively manage and work through the personal and human side of change. The model identifies three stages a person experiences during change: Ending what currently is, the Neutral Zone, and the New Beginning. [80]

Ending: Transition starts with an ending. Ironic, but true. This first phase of transition begins when people identify what they are losing and learn how to manage these losses. They determine what is over and being left behind, and what they will keep. These may include relationships, processes, team members, or locations.

The Neutral Zone: The second step of transition comes after letting go. People go through an in-between time when the old is gone but the new isn't fully known. The Neutral Zone is the very core of the transition process, when the critical psychological realignments and re-patterning take place. This is the time between the old reality and sense of identity and the new reality. In this zone, people are beginning to create new processes and learning what their new roles will be. They are in flux and may feel confusion and distress. The neutral zone is the seedbed for new beginnings.

New Beginnings: Involve new understandings, values, and attitudes. Beginnings are marked by a release of energy in a new direction. They are an expression of a fresh identity. Well-managed transitions allow people to establish new roles with an understanding of their purpose and the part they play and learn how to contribute and participate most effectively. As a result, they feel reoriented and renewed and are able to write themselves into the story.

In our work with leaders and organizations, we illustrate these three phases in the following graphic and describe the phases of transition in terms that leaders can visualize.

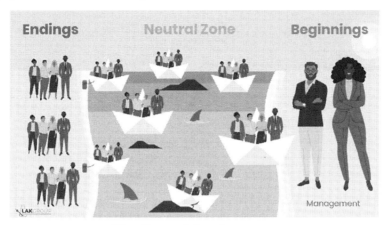

The Transition Journey

As you look at this diagram, you'll see Endings on the left side. This is the old life before the change, what needs to stop or go away. You'll see that there are several people that are waiting as if nothing is changing and some that haven't untied their boats to start their transition journey.

In the middle of the graphic, you'll find the Neutral Zone. As mentioned before, these individuals have let go of the old, accepted things that are ending, and have begun their journey into the unknown. That journey will consist of obstacles, challenges, and in some cases, some moves backward. (Note the boat caught up on the rocks.) The Neutral Zone is also a time for the flourishing of creativity because people are not holding on to either the old or the new yet.

Next, you'll see that one boat has landed in the Beginnings side of the diagram. Those people have made the transition through the Neutral Zone and are now ready to have the "new" be their own "new."

Finally, you'll notice that the management team is deeper inland in the Beginnings. This is because of the head start they had. The key here for leaders is to stop frequently and look back to see where everyone else is in their transition journey and find ways to help others let go and emerge from the Neutral Zone to New Beginnings. It doesn't do anyone any good if leadership keeps moving forward but doesn't have anyone following them

Leaders need to meet each individual where they are and lead them through their unique transition journey. Without doing that, they will face the cold reality that President

Franklin Delano Roosevelt describes in this quote: *"It is a terrible thing to look over your shoulder when you are trying to lead – and find no one there."*

Leading Others Through Change and Transition

Leading others through a significant change has both practical and emotional elements that impact each person's ability to transition. The difficult part for leaders is that each individual will manage change differently. In our research and practice, we have synthesized Six Best Practices when leading others through change and transition. Leaders who master these six steps will increase their effectiveness in helping lead through transitions.

1. **Communicate, Communicate, Communicate**

    Be transparent at all times. Share what you can, when you can. Help others understand what the change is and why it is happening. Don't stop with one announcement. Say the same thing multiple times and in different ways so people have a chance to hear it when they are ready to hear it. Use multiple modes, such as in person with individuals and with groups, emails, discussions, and newsletters. Watch and listen to everything. Respond to what you are seeing and hearing.

2. **Be Available**

    Make others the priority. Have an open door and strive to create a safe environment for anyone who comes to you. Be present and available when you are needed, not just when you have time.

3. **Clarify Expectations and Set Goals**

    Ensure that people understand what is expected of them. Set both short-term goals and milestones and celebrate when those are achieved. Hold people accountable and include behavior and tasks in the expectations. Walk the talk to set a good example for others to follow. Also, remember to check your Leadership Shadow. (See Chapter 4)

4. **Meet People Where They Are on Their Journey**

    Identify and acknowledge where others are in their transition journey and what they need from you. Provide what they need if possible; compensate if need be. Be inclusive and keep everyone in your line of sight. Be patient with where they are in their transition journey.

5. **Share Constructive and Positive Feedback**

   Acknowledge and celebrate when something has been done well. Give feedback individually and to the group when appropriate. Be timely in giving positive feedback and give constructive feedback as needed, offering alternatives when possible. People will appreciate the attention and support.

6. **Honor the Past**

   Pushing through change and transitioning to New Beginnings doesn't mean forgetting where you came from or where others came from and what you and others have been through. If you don't honor the past, it can cause others to wonder why they needed to change previously or, worse yet, if they were doing something wrong. You and your team can honor the past by:

   Learning from it. Identify what worked and what didn't work and how those lessons can be applied to the new situation.

   Respecting it. Don't talk badly about it. Be considerate of the past and those that contributed to it.

   Marking it. Have domain over it. Lock it up, toss it out, replace it, burn it, or take a piece of it.

   Transitioning from it. Show how it leads to the new. Acknowledge that it too was "the new" at one time.

Agile Leaders embolden themselves and encourage others to accept that the place they're leaving behind will always be part of their journey story, but the new path and destiny they're embarking on and the place they'll soon find themselves are completely within their command and capability.

Guiding the Organization

As we shared at the onset of this chapter, Agile Leaders can more effectively lead others through the transition process by first building up their own change-resilience. Only then can they begin to build that mindset and resiliency in others. Yet the vision and intention of an Agile Leader doesn't end there. The ultimate goal is to build and sustain a growth-oriented organization that is resilient to change. To that end, we're not talking solely about managing the process.

There are many different models on change management and they're all foundation-ally strong. What most model developers miss though is the significance of leadership and ensuring the ecosystem is growth-oriented, aligned to the vision, and resilient to change. We describe it as a culture resilient to change.

John Kotter's *Leading Change* doesn't focus on the process elements of change but rather on the organizational and leadership elements. He identifies the common errors made by leaders and outlines eight measures leaders must guide their organization through to achieve its goals. Kotter provides a practical resource for leaders and managers charged with making change initiatives work. [81]

1. **Establish a sense of urgency.** People need to know why they must change. This sense of urgency needs to be there constantly. Employees need to see themselves not as victims, but able to control the issues ("We can do this") and not hide behind external factors that dis-empower them.

2. **Create a guiding coalition.** No *one* individual can do it all alone – s/he needs to inspire a team who want to follow that vision and spread the word. The whole organization needs to feel responsible for change – everyone is an agent of change.

3. **Develop a vision and strategy.** Having a clear vision and strategy directs, aligns, and inspires action in all employees. The 'Vision story' needs to be constantly told – when you think you have told everyone, tell them again (and again…).

4. **Communicate the change vision.** Great visions are nothing if they cannot be communicated. Use stories/metaphors, multiple channels, simplicity, repetition, and leading by example.

5. **Empower employees for broad-based action.** Leaders need to help break through and find solutions and work-arounds to the organizational forces that prevent employees from making the changes required, such as silos, past values, lack of skills, old processes, department bosses with fixed mindsets, etc.

6. **Generate short-term wins.** It's critical to maintain the belief in and support for the change. Generating some quick wins helps to maintain belief, keeps the critics at bay, and refuels the momentum.

7. **Consolidate gains and produce more change.** Don't let the sense of urgency drop, as this is the point an organization can start to go backwards (as resistance is

always waiting to reassert itself). Create a more 'open system' where anyone can contribute ideas/raise issues/identify extra areas that need change.

8. **Anchor new approaches in the culture**. Get the new behaviors/ values/ beliefs firmly rooted. Change is never-ending, so leaders need to instill a culture resilient to constant change yet one that strives to learn, adapt, and grow.

Cultivating an Agile Culture

While Change Resiliency may be the final of the *Six Attributes of an Agile Leader*, it really is the key attribute in creating a growth-oriented, agile culture. Throughout our presentation of the six attributes thus far, we shared our best practices in cultivating Agile Leaders and developing skills and behaviors around:

Personal Integrity

Learning Agility

Coaching Others

Followership

Systems Thinking

Change Resiliency

The sum of all these attributes will help you to become a more effective, Agile Leader. Yet the story doesn't end there. Agile Leaders go on to anchor solid cultural norms that reflect the six attributes and, as a result, attract talented people who want to follow visionary and confident leaders they trust and who will allow them to grow and develop.

During uncertain times, colleagues and staff are watching leaders and how they lead through change and uncertainty. To become an employer of choice, organizations must establish a workplace that attracts, retains, and inspires top talent. This is created by leaders who lead *On Purpose*. Culture is an outcome created by leaders. It is the result of leadership behaviors and how they transcend through others in the organization.

Reflection Questions

- Are you comfortable working with ambiguity?
- When facing change, are you guided by an overarching commitment to your intentions?
- Do you avoid making decisions or changing for fear of failure?
- Is your tendency to proactively seek out and share information to build strength in self and others?
- Do people see you as a leader who uses a framework for thinking that challenges conventional wisdom and shows pathways?
- Are you able to embrace change as continuous improvement, unafraid of the future?

10
THE OUTCOME IS CULTURE

Culture is not an initiative. Culture is the enabler of all initiatives.

—*Larry Senn*

"We must change our culture!"
    "How can we sustain our cultural standards with so many people working remotely?"
    "What are we doing to make people more accountable for our culture?"

These are comments we often hear from senior leaders in companies of all shapes and sizes as they reflect on the cultures of their organizations. Interestingly, their employees tend to share different perceptions and expectations of their company's culture:

    "Management doesn't listen to us."
    "My manager gets it, but senior leaders don't understand."
    "People at the top need to come down and see how the rest of the company works."

We're also hearing novel views and expectations from Millennials and Gen Z – quite different from those of older generations who accepted whatever they received out of corporate life. "The company's culture" wasn't necessarily the top reason why the older generation worked for a company. Fast forward and here's what younger people are saying today.

    "I want to be a part of a company that has a culture where I can fit in and learn, develop, and grow."
    "I want to work for a company that has high integrity and includes its people in running the company."
    "I want to belong to a company that has purpose, that does great things for the community and that treats people fairly and equitably."

These concerns and beliefs will continue to be held by employees across all industries until leaders begin to accept that culture is the result of their own attitudes and behaviors, especially those of mid-level leaders. They're the ones (not senior leadership) who personally interact with practically every facet of an organization.

Mid-level leaders are the glue who encourage employee engagement and involvement, enrich the customer service experience, and build productive relationships with partners and suppliers. Leaders at all levels are responsible for creating the outcome called culture.

We began our book by defining what it means to Lead *On Purpose*, and we defined the foundational mindset of a leader who embraces and allows the Six Attributes of Agile Leadership to take root and develop.

So why does this matter? Companies today are looking to develop agile business strategies to contend with disruptive change. They need Agile Leaders who have followership and will inspire and support their talented workforce through changing times and keep them aligned, resilient, and centered on achieving their business objectives.

Agile Leaders can create cultures that sustain outcomes, increase engagement, retain top talent, and make you an employer of choice. Agile Leaders foster collaboration, build high performing teams, and drive consistent results. They're found to have deep personal integrity, a willingness to learn from experience, and the confidence and competence to translate that knowledge into action. They're resilient and maintain positive outlooks during the inevitable changes found in business and in life.

Culture is the outcome based on how leaders lead. A positive, engaging culture is the outcome of strong leadership capability and presence. It's not an activity or strategy that can be deployed. It's the result of cumulative and repetitive leadership actions and the impact and influence of those actions on the mindset of an organization's workforce. There are many examples of culture as the outcome of the attitudes, behaviors, and actions of an organization's leaders.

Creating a Culture of Caring

The name DaVita is an adaptation of the Italian phrase, "Giving Life." This is what teammates strive to do for DaVita patients every day, whether they work in a DaVita clinic, as a case manager, or as an accountant.

DaVita Medical Group, is one of the leading independent medical groups in the United States, providing kidney dialysis services through a network of outpatient dialysis centers globally. Leadership believed that they had to completely shape their culture to both change how they were being perceived in the marketplace and how they perceived each other as teammates.

DaVita's leadership created the "Village" to see themselves and project themselves as a community first and a company second.

They define their culture as The DaVita Way:

> *"We dedicate our Head, Heart and Hands to pursue the Mission, live the Values and build a healthy Village. It means that we care for each other with the same intensity with which we care for our patients. We believe that by caring for each other we can improve health care, grow leaders and make a real difference in the communities we serve."*[82]

The *On Purpose* leadership exhibited at DaVita encourages employees to care for each other and work toward a common good. To keep communication open and transparent, the company's senior leaders host town hall meetings where any teammate can ask any question of leadership.

DaVita's mission is to be the Provider, Partner, and Employer of Choice. Their vision is "To build the greatest health care community the world has ever seen," and all seven of their Core Values were voted on by DaVita teammates.

Leaders *On Purpose* have a passion for doing the right thing for people because they know the impact is going to be positive on the organization. They know that if they act in the right way, people will follow.

Becoming an Embracing Brand

Each year, the publication 24/7 Wall St. identifies 10 American brands that they predict will disappear before the end of the next year, and in 2014, they chose athletic clothing retailer Lululemon as one of the 10 that would fail.[83]

It was hard to believe, because in 2014, Lululemon – a brand known for its expensive yoga pants, expensive yoga classes, costly spinning workouts, and treadmills in $200-a-month gyms in upscale neighborhoods – was the ninth most valuable clothing brand in the world.[84]

One of the reasons they were not expected to survive was because of the mounting lawsuits emanating from their degradation of women who were heavier in size. You see, Lululemon's culture was defined by its controversial founder and CEO who actually blamed women's bodies for their yoga pants not performing well. Something needed to change, because leadership was driving the athletic clothier into the ground. A great product and brilliant marketing can't help a company if its messaging to its customers is disparaging and its employees consider the company's culture "toxic" and its leaders as showing "no accountability."[85]

New leadership came in and completely changed the culture and led them back to success. Lululemon announced that it was redesigning legging length, color, and silhouette; adding four new pant styles; and categorizing them by fit. Consumers are now able to purchase leggings that make them feel good about themselves. Rather than shaming women for being too big or having the wrong body, Lululemon has changed its culture to embracing physical differences and now offers a diverse range of clothes that help women feel *better* about their bodies.

The new leaders created an environment where employees could prosper and the brand could grow, and the product symbolizes the new culture they were hoping to create. It all started with a change of leadership and the attitudes and actions of *On Purpose* leaders. That's what drove the new culture of Lululemon and led to them becoming the brand that they are today with a culture that will sustain that performance for a long time to come.

The Agile Leader Creates the Outcome

Companies such as DiVita and Lululemon 'forming' themselves into a desired outcome is an intense and intentional culture shaping process that begins with the behaviors expected from the leaders in the organization.

Many times, senior leaders will express a desire to jump right in and start shaping their culture based on something they experienced or heard about or a company they'd like to emulate. We believe the most important and productive first step forward is to step back and understand the current state of your culture and where you intend for your organization to go.

Begin with the End in Mind

When building the culture of an organization toward a desired outcome, you have to begin with the end in mind. Results must be the ultimate focus, for they're the product of the adopted behaviors demonstrated by others in the organization. As the following graph illustrates, the behaviors people demonstrate are motivated by the beliefs they hold, which are reinforced by their experiences.

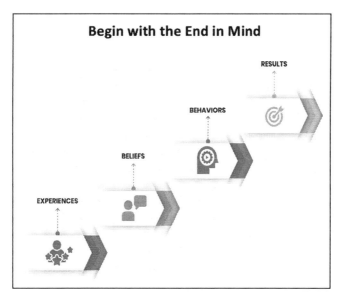

With the end in mind, leaders have a responsibility to create a different reality. When employees start **Experiencing** something different, it will influence their **Beliefs** – what they deem to be true about their experiences and their current reality. The change in beliefs will then lead to demonstrating different **Behaviors** – behaviors that are more in line with what is desired and needed in order to achieve the end **Results**.

One of our clients was working on changing the way they recruit, select, and onboard new talent to the organization. They were getting feedback that candidates were not happy with the process and the communication they received.

In our project kick-off meeting, our client immediately started down a path of solutions and process changes. One leader even suggested a new organization design for recruitment to solve the problem.

We asked, "*What is the candidate experience you hope to achieve with this process?*"

There were initially blank stares around the table and then a variety of ideas sprung up on what the candidate experience should be – though none were linked to any of the current processes or practices at the organization.

The team decided to take a different direction, beginning with the gathering of data on the current candidate experience. This led to a discussion on the expected results, followed by a focus on the beliefs and expected behaviors that the organization needed to achieve the outcomes.

Today, the timeline for hiring is 45 percent faster than the organization's historical norms. Candidates feel engaged immediately in the process and survey ratings on candidate experience are consistently in the 90 percent satisfaction range. Hiring managers are happy with improved transparency in communication as well as greater clarity on the process and in the role each person plays.

To shape the results of an organization, Agile Leaders create new experiences that create and reinforce desired beliefs and practices. This in turn drives new behaviors and builds momentum toward achieving the desired results. When leaders begin by thinking about experiences and then work their way through beliefs and behaviors, results are achieved faster and more efficiently, and most importantly, results are sustained.

Agile Leaders who tap into the hearts and minds of their team members and paint an inspirational picture of success confidently, competently, and trustingly give their people and others in the organization something to hold on to and to work toward. It also creates a powerful opportunity for everyone to write themselves into the story.

Your Shadow Speaks and People Are Watching

In Chapter 4, we shared the importance of Personal Integrity and the shadows cast by leaders that have a huge impact on whether people will follow those leaders. A leader's shadow can strengthen a company's culture and the engagement and commitment of its employees. People can tell if you're a leader who leads *On Purpose*. They can tell if you're committed to what you're trying to do and if you're there to support them, versus someone who's just managing the process and playing through.

On Purpose leaders must own and lead the behaviors that shape the culture of an organization. They're accountable for creating the experiences of employees, customers, and the communities they serve. This is the badge of honor that comes with being a leader. The reality is that organizations become "Shadows of their Leaders."

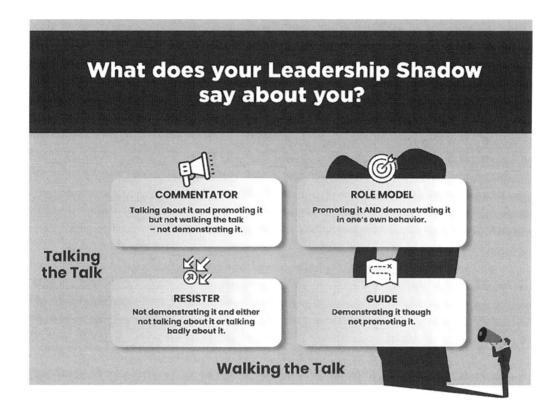

It's a heavy burden to consider for people who want to be leaders. They have to navigate shifting landscapes, changing markets, a demanding workforce, and expectations of boards and outside constituents. It is a bit of a cliché to say that they must "adapt and overcome," but that is one of many sayings that are simply realities that have proven themselves over time.

One of the more important aspects of the Shadow of a Leader is that people will watch and follow you. Sometimes they won't even be aware of what they are doing. Your attitudes and behaviors become *their* attitudes and behaviors.

The best examples of this mirroring are found in our personal lives. Sons and daughters watch and emulate their fathers and mothers – the most influential people in their young lives. This brings to mind the song, *Boy*, by American singer-songwriter Lee Brice, about a son who is going to be great because he does what his dad does.[86]

Boy, you're gonna know it all
You'll think you're ten feet tall …
You're gonna drop the ball

Hit the wall …
I know you will, 'cause you're a part of me
And a part of you will always be a boy

We believe leaders are like dads and moms. People watch them and follow them. They want their boss to be happy with how they're performing. They'll mirror how their leaders behave, because if they do that, they know that they're probably going to connect with their leaders and be viewed favorably.

We've met leaders and up-coming leaders who, upon learning about the influence of their shadow, will shy away from assuming the burden or deny their influence altogether. Basketball legend Charles Barkley once boldly declared to the media that he was not a role model and that kids should be taught to emulate their parents, not athletes or celebrities.[87]

The reality is that if you're in a position of influence, people are going to emulate you – whether you want them to or not. Leaders are role models, and we believe that if you're going to be a leader, you need to be one who leads *On Purpose*. You need to become the model of behavior that others will trust, emulate, and follow. It's then a matter of what you want your shadow to reflect.

Getting to Great

We were recently asked by a senior leadership team if we could help them shape aspects of their company's culture. This particular company had a legacy of strong cultural norms, such as high-performance expectations, committed, hard-working employees, solid foundational core values, and a history of good business performance.

The leadership team felt they had room to improve and genuinely wanted to be great, not simply good. They had a strong belief that better collaboration across the organization would create greater alignment among their portfolio of business units. Leading up to this declaration was the leadership team's acknowledgement that most of their organization-wide initiatives had fallen short of potential, namely two major undertakings:

- A new and expensive technology platform didn't yield the results it could have.
- A major acquisition that would have nearly doubled the size of the organization fell through once they realized the integration of the two companies was not going to materialize.

As we started to assess the current state of the existing culture, it became clear that the company had "We/They" issues and turf conflicts between corporate and the business units and among the different business units themselves. They were playing a game of win/lose instead of win/win within their own organization.

It didn't take long to realize that the issues centered largely on the behaviors of the senior leadership team. They were not fully aligned or mutually supportive, and this negative shadow was cast over their teams and ultimately enveloped the entire organization. As an example, leaders were "generally nice" to each other and non-confrontational during executive team meetings, but would not support the decisions and initiatives after the meetings.

As we dug deeper, we found that many of the same behaviors existed at the second level of leaders who reported directly to senior team members. When we asked people at lower levels in the organization why they didn't collaborate better, this comment reflected how most felt …

"Why should we? Our bosses don't."

Leaders casting a shadow that others observe and follow is without question a heavy burden for those who care, have a vision, and intend to bear that burden. Leaders *On Purpose* understand the nature of the role, accept it, and revel in the opportunity to shape the direction of their organization and positively influence others.

Throughout the book, we have shared many best practices, models, steps, and thoughts that leaders can take to be more agile, lead *On Purpose*, and ultimately be more effective. The question is, how does one best develop the requisite skills and perspectives?

At the end of the day, development activities cannot be an island. Efforts to develop others –whether formal or informal – cannot exist as stand-alone or one-off initiatives. Rather, development needs to be an interstate that runs through everything, with off and on ramps at key points in an individual's journey to becoming a more effective Agile Leader.

Align on a Plan Prior to Starting the Journey

When embarking on a trip, people seldom simply jump in the car or hop on a plane and just go somewhere. They typically have a destination in mind and some idea as to how they're going to get to where they want to go and what they'll do once they get there. People development efforts should be thought of in the same light.

Preparation begins by first understanding that the direction of development will change, as will the method of development. Therefore, to get started with the greatest chance of success, leaders need to understand where they are headed, for what reason, and how it's connected to everything else they're doing at work on a daily basis.

When thinking about leadership development, we encourage an approach that looks at the three pieces we've been discussing throughout our book: the organization, its individual leaders, and others in the organization.

First, the organization needs to define the talent and skills it needs in order to be successful in meeting the future needs of the organization. Identifying those characteristics, experiences, aspirations, and traits (both professionally and personally) ahead of time will help drive the direction and development of individual leaders within the organization.

Secondly, leaders need to look at themselves, work with others to identify what they want their future to look like, and then work within the organization to achieve those desired results. Identifying how they can further develop to continue to add value to the organization – as well as to continue to grow themselves – is a win/win for everyone involved.

Finally, when considering leadership development, the responsibility that a leader has for the development of others must be the primary goal. This is the key to the sustainability and the future success of the organization. Focus on adaptive learning practices. Coaching is a great example. This enables the leader to adapt the content and experience based on his/her needs.

Organizations talk about wanting to shape, redefine, or transform their culture. Too often, this means initiating a "culture changing activity" that often fails to lead to any sustainable change.

Culture is an outcome – not an initiative.

Any culture change initiative must focus on the following:
- Expectations of leaders and all employees
- What is and isn't acceptable behavior
- Identifying inhibitors and removing them
- What the reward is for aligning behaviors with those expectations
- Clearly stating and following through on the consequences for behaving in ways that do not align with what's acceptable
- Inspiring every employee to write themselves in to the company story
- Shaping how leaders are going to "show up" each and every day

How organizations bring these elements to life creates the culture – the outcome of what is and is not rewarded and tolerated within an organization.

To create a change in how people act and ultimately build a sustainable business model, leaders need to know that their behaviors matter and that they're responsible for more than processes or tasks. They need to Lead *On Purpose*.

On Purpose leaders are trusted, followed, and even admired. They cast a positive shadow that often endures well beyond their time in office. They serve as a catalyst for change and an anchor for core principals and direction.

Our challenge to you is to look within yourself and ask, with all sincerity, *"Why do I want to be a leader?"* Understand what you're hoping to not just attain for yourself by being in that role, but what you hope to contribute to others and the organization. We can all think of both great and bad leaders in our lives. By being mindful of good intent, we try to mirror the behaviors of the good ones and shun the behaviors of the bad. How do you want your leadership to be regarded by others? What shadow do you want to cast?

Our hope for you is that you've gained insights into how you can be a more Agile Leader and more consistently Lead *On Purpose*. We hope that you've found the inspiration within these pages to find your purpose and the ideas and roadmaps to develop the important attributes of your agile leadership.

We hope that you'll continue to develop and create environments that allow others to grow and develop as well. We also hope that you will inspire them to tap into *their* purpose in the work they do, and in doing so, you'll enable them to write themselves into the story.

REFERENCES

1   Dweck, Carol S. (2007). *Mindset: The New Psychology of Success.* New York: Ballantine Books. p 99. Retrieved from https://www.amazon.com/Mindset-Psychology-Carol-S-Dweck/dp/0345472322/ref=sr_1_1?dchild=1&keywords=Carol+Dweck&qid=1592251266&sr=8-1

2   Jardins, Julie Des (October, 2011). *Madame Curie's Passion*, Smithsonian. Retrieved from https://www.smithsonianmag.com/history/madame-curies-passion-74183598/

3   Freiberg, Kevin and Jackie (January 4, 2019). *20 Reasons Why Herb Kelleher Was One of The Most Beloved Leaders of Our Time.* Forbes. Retrieved from https://www.forbes.com/sites/kevinandjackiefreiberg/2019/01/04/20-reasons-why-herb-kelleher-was-one-of-the-most-beloved-leaders-of-our-time/#413fb1feb311

4   Ibid

5   The Ritz-Carlton Leadership Center (March 19, 2019). *The Power of Empowerment.* Retrieved from https://ritzcarltonleadershipcenter.com/2019/03/19/the-power-of-empowerment/

6   Lipman, Victor, (May 9, 2017). *Why Confidence Is a Leader's Best Friend.* Forbes. Retrieved from https://www.forbes.com/sites/victorlipman/2017/05/09/why-confidence-is-always-a-leaders-best-friend/#2c1cb0d647be

7   Stallard, Mike (May 16, 2015). *Michael Jordan's Transformation Contributed to His Success.* Connection Culture Group. Retrieved from https://www.connectionculture.com/post/michael-jordans-transformation-contributed-to-his-success

8   The Disney Institute. *Leadership Lessons from Walt Disney: Communicating a Vision.* Retrieved from https://www.disneyinstitute.com/blog/leadership-lessons-from-walt-disney-communicating-a-vision/

9   Mohler, Albert R. Jr. (November 2015). *The Conviction to Lead: Winston Churchill's Courageous Legacy.* Southern Equip. Retrieved from https://equip.sbts.edu/publications/towers/the-courageous-and-convictional-leadership-of-winston-churchill/

10 Heshmat, Shahram, Ph.D. (April 23, 2015). *What is Confirmation Bias?* Psychology Today. Retrieved from https://www.psychologytoday.com/us/blog/science-choice/201504/what-is-confirmation-bias

11 Thetell Blog, (February 3, 2014). *Wells Fargo Tops List of Most Valuable Banking Brands*. Market Watch. Retrieved from https://www.marketwatch.com/story/wells-fargo-tops-list-of-most-valuable-banking-brands-1391456457

12 Bariso, Justin. (September 13, 2013). *How Could 5,000 Employees Cheat? The Science Behind the Wells Fargo Scandal*. Inc. Retrieved from https://www.inc.com/justin-bariso/why-cheaters-cheat-the-science-behind-the-wells-fargo-scandal.html

13 Carucci, Ron (November 13, 2007). *Executives Fail to Execute Strategy Because They're Too Internally Focused*. Harvard Business Review. Retrieved from https://hbr.org/2017/11/executives-fail-to-execute-strategy-because-theyre-too-internally-focused

14 ibid

15 The Caliper Profile. Retrieved from https://calipercorp.com/caliper-profile/

16 Ibid

17 Sturt, David, & Nordstrom, Todd (March 8, 2018). 10 Shocking Workplace Stats You Need to Know. Forbes. Retrieved from https://www.forbes.com/sites/davidsturt/2018/03/08/10-shocking-workplace-stats-you-need-to-know/#2f9ed25ef3af

18 Carucci, Ron (November 13, 2007). *Executives Fail to Execute Strategy Because They're Too Internally Focused*. Harvard Business Review. Retrieved from https://hbr.org/2017/11/executives-fail-to-execute-strategy-because-theyre-too-internally-focused

19 Tanveer Naseer Leadership. Becoming A Leader For All The Wrong Reasons. Retrieved from https://www.tanveernaseer.com/becoming-a-leader-for-all-the-wrong-reasons/

20 Ibid

21 Sturt, David, Nordstrom, Todd (March 8, 2018). *10 Shocking Workplace Stats You Need to Know*. Forbes. Retrieved from https://www.forbes.com/sites/davidsturt/2018/03/08/10-shocking-workplace-stats-you-need-to-know/#2f9ed25ef3af

22 Gallup Research (2015). *State of the American Manager: Analytics and Advice for Leaders*. Retrieved from https://www.aseonline.org/images/marketing/StateOfAmericanManager_Gallup.pdf

23 ibid

24 Maxwell, John C. (September, 2007). *The 21 Irrefutable Laws of Leadership: Follow Them and People Will follow You*. New York: Harper Collins. Retrieved from https://www.amazon.com/21-Irrefutable-Laws-Leadership-Anniversary/dp/0785288376/ref=sr_1_1?dchild=1&keywords=21+Irrefutable+Laws+of+Leadership&qid

=1593800607&sr=8-1

25 Hallenbeck, George (April 6, 2017). *How to Use Experience to Fuel Leadership Development*. Center for Creative Leadership. Retrieved from https://www.ccl.org/blog/use-experience-fuel-leadership-development/

26 Swisher, Vicki and Dai, Guangrong (June 3, 2015). *The Agile Enterprise: Taking Stock of Learning Agility to Gauge the Fit of the Talent Pool to the Strategy*. Korn Ferry Institute. Retrieved from https://www.td.org/insights/learning-agility-prime-indicator-of-business-success

27 Goldsmith, Margie (October 30, 2017). *Everything but the Kitchen Sink: The Kohler Family Dynasty on Governance, Next Gens, and Philanthropy*. Camden FB. Retrieved from http://www.campdenfb.com/article/everything-kitchen-sink-kohler-family-dynasty-governance-next-gens-and-philanthropy

28 Zak, Paul J. (January-February 2017). *The Neuroscience of Trust*, Harvard Business Review. Retrieved from https://hbr.org/2017/01/the-neuroscience-of-trust

29 ibid

30 Johnson, M. K., Rowatt, W. C., & Petrini, L. (2011). *A New Trait on the Market: Honesty- Humility as a Unique Predictor of Job Performance Ratings*. Personality and Individual Differences. pp 50, 857-862. Retrieved from https://www.sciencedirect.com/science/article/abs/pii/S0191886911000146

31 Palanski, M. E., & Yammarino, F. J. (2011). *Impact of Behavioral Integrity on Follower Job Performance: A Three-study Examination*. The Leadership Quarterly, 22, 765-786. Retrieved from https://www.sciencedirect.com/science/article/pii/S1048984311000683

32 Dineen, B. R., Lewicki, R. J., Tomlinson, E. C. (2006). *Supervisory Guidance and Behavioral Integrity: Relationships with Employee Citizenship and Deviant Behavior*. Journal of Applied Psychology, 91, 622-635. Retrieved from https://psycnet.apa.org/record/2006-07101-009

33   Dirks, K. T., Ferrin, D. L. (2002). *Trust in Leadership: Meta-analytic Findings and Implications for Research and Practice.* Journal of Applied Psychology, 87, 611-628. Retrieved from https://ink.library.smu.edu.sg/cgi/viewcontent.cgi?article=1674&context=lkcsb_research

34   PBS, *Character Above All Essays*: Stephen Ambrose on Dwight D. Eisenhower. Retrieved from https://www.pbs.org/newshour/spc/character/essays/eisenhower.html

35   Pricewaterhouse Coopers 19th Annual Global CEO Survey (January 2016). *Redefining Business Success in a Changing World.* Retrieved from https://www.pwc.com/gx/en/ceo-survey/2016/landing-page/pwc-19th-annual-global-ceo-survey.pdf

36   ibid

37   ibid

38   Google Research (2016). *Understanding Team Effectiveness.* Retrieved from https://rework.withgoogle.com/print/guides/5721312655835136/

39   Schulman, Miriam (December 1, 2001). *Coming to Grips with Guilt: A White-Collar Felon Reflects on His Crime.* Markkula Center for Applied Ethics, Santa Clara University. Retrieved from https://www.scu.edu/ethics/focus-areas/business-ethics/resources/coming-to-grips-with-guilt-a-white-collar-felon/

40   Ibid

41   Gariano, Fransesca (March 29, 2020). *Columbia Sportswear CEO Cuts Salary to $10K, Keeps Paying Employees Regular Wages.* Today. Retrieved from https://www.today.com/style/columbia-sportswear-ceo-cuts-salary-10-000-t177055

42   Sokolowski, Alexandre (May 5, 2005). *The Day Andy Roddick's Sportsmanship Cost Him Victory. Tennis Majors.* Retrieved from https://www.tennismajors.com/our-features/on-this-day/may-5-2005-the-day-andy-roddicks-sportsmanship-cost-him-victory-210307.html

43   Global Workplace Analytics (June 2020). *Work-At-Home After COVID-19—Our Forecast.* Retrieved from https://globalworkplaceanalytics.com/work-at-home-after-covid-19-our-forecast

44   ibid

45   The McKinsey Agile Tribe (January 22, 2018). *The Five Trademarks of an Agile Organization. McKinsey & Company*. Retrieved from https://www.mckinsey.com/business-functions/organization/our-insights/the-five-trademarks-of-agile-organizations#

46   ibid

47   Smith, David Dr. (May 31, 2018). *Developing Learning Ability*. Learning Vignettes. Retrieved from https://vignettestraining.blogspot.com/2018/05/4-ways-to-develop-learning-agility-tip.html

48   Korn Ferry Lominger (2017). *The Organizational X-Factor: Learning Agility*. Leadership and Talent. Retrieved from https://focus.kornferry.com/leadership-and-talent/the-organisational-x-factor-learning-agility/

49   Korn Ferry Lominger (2015). *FYI® For Learning Agility*. Retrieved from https://www.kornferry.com/content/dam/kornferry/docs/article-migration//82199-FYI_Learning_Agility_2nd_BLAD.pdf

50   Dweck, Carol S. (2007). *Mindset: The New Psychology of Success*. New York: Ballantine Books. p 99. Retrieved from https://www.amazon.com/Mindset-Psychology-Carol-S-Dweck/dp/0345472322/ref=sr_1_1?dchild=1&keywords=Carol+Dweck&qid=1592251266&sr=8-1

51   Mindset Works (2017). *Decades of Scientific Research that Started a Growth Mindset Revolution*. Retrieved from https://www.mindsetworks.com/about-us/default

52   Livengood, Chad (May 17, 2020). *Trump to Tour Ford's Ventilator Assembly Plant in Ypsilanti on Thursday*. Crain's Detroit Business. Retrieved from https://www.crainsdetroit.com/coronavirus/trump-tour-fords-ventilator-assembly-plant-ypsilanti-thursday

53   The McKinsey Agile Tribe (January 22, 2018). *The Five Trademarks of an Agile Organization*. McKinsey & Company. Retrieved from https://www.mckinsey.com/business-functions/organization/our-insights/the-five-trademarks-of-agile-organizations#

54   Maxwell, John C., (September, 2007). *The 21 Irrefutable Laws of Leadership: Follow Them and People Will follow You*. New York: Harper Collins. Retrieved from https://www.amazon.com/21-Irrefutable-Laws-Leadership-Anniversary/dp/0785288376/ref=sr_1_1?dchild=1&keywords=21+Irrefutable+Laws+of+Leadership&qid=1593800607&sr=8-1

55   Eliason, Nat (August 4, 2017). *The Perfect Time to Get a Mentor.* Better Humans. Retrieved from https://medium.com/better-humans/the-perfect-time-to-get-a-mentor-a93d6dce061e

56   ibid

57   ibid

58   Stanier, Michael Bungay (February 29, 2020) *The Advice Trap: Be Humble, Stay Curious & Change the Way You Lead Forever.* Vancouver: Page Two Publishing, p 5-7. Retrieved from https://www.amazon.com/dp/1989025757/ref=rdr_ext_tmb

59   ibid

60   Marquardt, Michael J. (February 17, 2014). *Leading with Questions: How Leaders Find the Right Solutions by Knowing What to Ask.* San Francisco: Jossey-Bass, p 19. Retrieved from https://www.amazon.com/Leading-Questions-Leaders-Solutions-Knowing/dp/1118658132/ref=sr_1_1?dchild=1&keywords=Leading+with+Questions&qid=1598364519&sr=8-1

61   AMA Staff (January 24, 2019). *When to Coach and When Not To.* American Management Association. Retrieved from https://www.amanet.org/articles/when-to-coach-and-when-not-to/

62   Wallenfeldt, Jeff (August 3, 2020). *John Lewis: American Civil Rights Leader and Politician.* Britannica. Retrieved from https://www.britannica.com/biography/John-Lewis-American-civil-rights-leader-and-politician

63   ibid

64   Covey, Stephen M. R., (February 5, 2008). *The Speed of Trust: The One Thing That Changes Everything.* FranklinCovey Publishing. p 13-14. Retrieved from https://www.amazon.com/SPEED-TRUST-Thing-Changes-Everything/dp/1416549005/ref=sr_1_3?dchild=1&keywords=speed+of+trust&qid=1599755419&sr=8-3

65   Crowley, Mark, C. (November 9, 2012). *The Leadership Genius of Abraham Lincoln.* Retrieved from https://www.fastcompany.com/3002803/leadership-genius-abraham-lincoln

66   The John Maxwell Company (July 10, 2013). *Gain Respect, Gain Followers: Six Ways to Gain the Respect of Others.* Retrieved from https://www.johnmaxwell.com/blog/gain-respect-gain-followers-6-ways-to-gain-others-respect/

67   ibid

68   NCS Coaching, *Leadership Quality: Seeing the Bigger Picture.* The Happy Manager. Retrieved from https://the-happy-manager.com/articles/leadership-quality/

69   Biology Online. *Ecosystem Definition.* Retrieved from https://www.biologyonline.com/dictionary/ecosystem

70   Martin, Sharon LCSW (August 18, 2019). *The Martyr Complex: How to Stop Feeling Like a Victim and Create Healthy Relationships.* Psych Central. Retrieved from https://blogs.psychcentral.com/imperfect/2016/10/martyr-complex-how-to-stop-feeling-like-a-victim-create-healthy-relationships/

71   Narcissism, Toxic People. *Martyr Complex and Covert Narcissism: Everything You Need to Know.* Toxicities. Retrieved from https://toxicties.com/martyr-complex-covert-narcissism/

72   Friedman, Edward H., (May 14, 2017). *A Failure of Nerve, Revised Edition: Leadership in the Age of the Quick Fix.* New York: Church Publishing. pp 13-14 Retrieved from https://www.amazon.com/Failure-Nerve-Revised-Leadership-Quick/dp/1596272791/ref=sr_1_1?dchild=1&keywords=A+Failure+of+Nerve&qid=1602103276&sr=8-1

73   Ollhoff, Jim, Walcheski. *Making the Jump to Systems Thinking.* The Systems Thinker. Retrieved from https://thesystemsthinker.com/making-the-jump-to-systems-thinking/

74   Orr, Evelyn, J., (March 12, 2012). *Becoming an Agile Leader: A Guide to Learning from Your Experiences,* Los Angeles: Korn Ferry Publishing, p 98. Retrieved from https://www.amazon.com/Becoming-Agile-Leader-Learning-Experiences-ebook/dp/B009ZMIAVA/ref=sr_1_3?dchild=1&keywords=Becoming+an+Agile+Leader%3A+A+Guide+to+Learning+from+Your+Experiences&qid=1602692878&sr=8-3

75   Pulley, Mary Lynn, Wakefield, Michael (August 22, 2002). *Building Resiliency How to Thrive in Times of Change.* Pfeiffer Publishing, p 7. Retrieved from https://www.amazon.com/Building-Resiliency-Thrive-Times-Change/dp/1882197674/ref=sr_1_3?dchild=1&keywords=How+to+Thrive+in+Times+of+Change&qid=1602184914&sr=8-3

76   Indigo Anchor (2018). *On the Origins of VUCA and How it Affects Decision Making.* Retrieved from https://www.indigoanchor.com/blog/2019/10/31/on-the-origins-of-vuca-and-how-it-affects-decision-making

77   ibid

78   Snowden, David J., Boone, Mary E. (September 2007). *A Leader's Framework for Decision Making.* Harvard Business Review. Retrieved from https://hbr.org/2007/11/a-leaders-framework-for-decision-making

79   ibid

80   Bridges, William (December 17, 2019). *Transitions: Making Sense of Life's Changes.* Boston: Da Capo Lifelong Books. Retrieved from https://www.amazon.com/Transitions-Making-Sense-Lifes-Changes/dp/0738285404/ref=sr_1_1?crid=2S7UPTBH-DR6V0&dchild=1&keywords=transitions+by+william+bridges&qid=1602706818&sprefix=transitions%2Caps%2C169&sr=8-1

81   Kotter, John P., (November 6, 2012). *Leading Change.* Boston: Harvard Business Review Press. Retrieved from https://www.amazon.com/Leading-Change-New-Preface-Author/dp/1422186431/ref=sr_1_2?dchild=1&keywords=leading+change&qid=1602782971&sr=8-2

82   DaVita/Careers. Retrieved from https://careers.davita.com/davitaculture

83   Wilbur, Hayley (September 4, 2015). *How Much More Does Lululemon Have to Fail Before Customers Bail?* Mashable. Retrieve from https://mashable.com/2015/09/04/lululemon-price-increase/

84   McIntyre, Douglas, A. (July 8, 2014). *10 Brands That Will Disappear in 2015.* 27/7 Wall St. Retrieved from https://247wallst.com/special-report/2014/07/08/10-brands-that-will-disappear-in-2015/

85   Lieber, Chavie (February 14, 2018). *Lululemon Employees Report a Toxic "Boy's Club" Culture.* Racked. Retrieved from https://www.racked.com/2018/2/14/17007924/lululemon-work-culture-ceo-laurent-potdevin

86   Brice, Lee. *Boy.* Song Facts. Retrieved from https://www.songfacts.com/facts/lee-brice/boy

87   Eisenberg, Jeff (July 17, 2019). *Iconic Spots Commercials: Charles Barkley's 'I am not a role model'.* Yahoo online. Retrieved from https://www.yahoo.com/now/iconic-sports-commercials-charles-barkleys-i-am-not-a-role-model-055726035.html

BIOGRAPHIES

Michael P. Grubich
President & Managing Partner - LAK Group

As a president and partner at the LAK Group, Michael Grubich brings more than 25 years of global leadership experience that enhances the performance of the organizations, individuals, teams, and leaders that he serves.

Michael helps organizations think strategically in order to move from concepts to practical implementation in all areas, from selection to succession. He provides consultation and coaching to senior leaders in order to help them move their businesses forward through an integrated approach of aligning talent, culture, and business objectives.

Prior to joining LAK Group, Michael served in several global thought and operational leadership roles at Aurora Health Care, CNH Industrial, Kohler Company, and Jockey International. During this time, he led a variety of human resources functions, including Talent Management, Leadership Development, Talent Acquisition, Succession Management, Learning and Development, Assessment, Change Management, Strategic Planning, and Engagement Practices.

Michael holds a Bachelor of Science degree from Northern Illinois University and earned his Master's degree in Business Administration (MBA) from Lake Forest Graduate School of Business. Outside of work, Mike serves as Secretary, Board of Directors for Special Olympics in Wisconsin, and is the Board Chair for Catholic Memorial High School in Waukesha, Wisconsin. He is also an adjunct faculty member at Marquette University's College of Business Administration.

Michael can be reached at: mgrubich@lak-group.com

Shelley A. Smith
Managing Director, Leadership Practice - LAK Group

Shelley joined LAK Group in 2019 with more than 20 years of experience in leadership, consulting with executives, and coaching and organizational development. Shelley's passion is to help leaders and organizations focus on purpose and talent in order to help move individuals and organizations forward.

Shelley's areas of expertise include executive coaching, physician leadership coaching, leadership/talent development, change and succession management, and performance consulting.

Prior to joining LAK Group, Shelley was part of the Talent and Organization Development team at Aurora Health Care, most recently serving in the Senior Director Leadership Development position. Her accomplishments at Aurora included the development of their Coaching Practice Center, receipt of the National Center for Healthcare Leadership's BOLD (Best Organizations in Leadership Development) Award, the build out and startup of a regional medical center campus, and multiple training programs and consulting initiatives focused on talent management, change management, physician leadership development, and organizational development. Shelley also spent 16 years in the financial services industry in various roles that included leading the training and development function, the financial and regulatory turnaround of a branch office, and the oversight of multiple professional teams.

Shelley holds a Bachelor of Science degree from the University of Wisconsin Stevens Point and a Master's in Business Administration from Concordia University of Wisconsin. She is proudly passionate about the credibility of the coaching profession, is a faculty member of the Coach Academy International, an ICF certified coach, is a Board Certified Coach (BCC), and is certified through The Physician Coaching Institute.

In her free time, Shelley enjoys spending time with her grandsons, her Mastiffs, and with her husband on their Harley Davidson seeing many beautiful local and national sights.

Shelley can be reached at: ssmith@lak-group.com

About LAK Group

At the LAK Group, we work with leaders to transform business goals into human strategies that put the right people in the right seats, so everyone wins – even as your market changes.

Our team of seasoned management consulting professionals has been in your shoes, so we understand the hurdles that you need to clear to get things done. That's why we create plans for culture, development, retention, and outplacement for a range of clients in a variety of industries.

Our services include:

Leadership Development
- Coaching
- Leadership Programs
- Developing Leaders as Coaches
- Dyad Leadership Development Program
- Nurse Leadership Program

Culture Shaping
- Culture Transformation
- Organization Design
- Change Resiliency

Career Transformation
- Outplacement Services
- Career Coaching
- Team Development

Talent Strategy
- Talent Alignment & Planning
- Assessments for Selection and Development
- Succession Management
- Strategic Planning & Visioning
- Talent Management Practices

Visit our website at www.lak-group.com

Follow us at www.linkedin.com/company/lakgroup/

LAK Group
375 Bishops Way, Suite 230
Brookfield, WI 53005
(262) 786-9200

Made in the USA
Columbia, SC
11 April 2021